CHANGE YOUR MIND

FREEDOM FROM IMMORAL THINKING

JEFF GOFORTH

CHANGE YOUR MIND

FREEDOM FROM IMMORAL THINKING

Change Your Mind: Freedom from Immoral Thinking
Copyright © 2016—Jeff Goforth
ISBN 978-0-9892257-9-3
Printed in the United States

Published by
Paladin Publishing
PO Box 700515
Tulsa, OK 74170

Unless otherwise indicated, all Scripture quotations are taken from the Holy Bible, New Living Translation, copyright © 1996, 2004, 2007, 2013, 2015 by Tyndale House Foundation. Used by permission of Tyndale House Publishers, Inc., Carol Stream, Illinois 60188. All rights reserved.

Scripture quotations from THE MESSAGE. Copyright © by Eugene H. Peterson 1993, 1994, 1995, 1996, 2000, 2001, 2002. Used by permission of NavPress. All rights reserved. Represented by Tyndale House Publishers, Inc.

Scriptures marked AMP are taken from the AMPLIFIED BIBLE (AMP): Scripture taken from the AMPLIFIED® BIBLE, Copyright © 1954, 1958, 1962, 1964, 1965, 1987 by the Lockman Foundation Used by permission. www.Lockman.org

Scriptures marked NKJV are taken from the NEW KING JAMES VERSION (NKJV): Scripture taken from the NEW KING JAMES VERSION®. Copyright© 1982 by Thomas Nelson, Inc. Used by permission. All rights reserved.

Scriptures marked TLB are taken from THE LIVING BIBLE (TLB): Scripture taken from THE LIVING BIBLE copyright© 1971. Used by permission of Tyndale House Publishers, Inc., Carol Stream, Illinois 60188. All rights reserved.

Scripture quotations marked AMPC are taken from the Amplified® Bible, Copyright © 1954, 1958, 1962, 1964, 1965, 1987 by The Lockman Foundation. Used by permission. www.Lockman.org

Scriptures marked NIV are taken from the NEW INTERNATIONAL VERSION (NIV): Scripture taken from THE HOLY BIBLE, NEW INTERNATIONAL VERSION ®. Copyright©1973, 1978, 1984, 2011 by Biblica, Inc.™. Used by permission of Zondervan.

All rights reserved. No part of this publication may be reproduced, stored in a retrieval system, or transmitted in any form or by any means—electronic, mechanical, photocopy, recording, scanning or other—except for brief quotations in critical reviews or articles without the prior written permission of the Publisher.

Development by PriorityPR Group & Literary Agency – www.prioritypr.org
Cover Design by Daniel Hook—www.danielhook.com
Text Design by Lisa Simpson — SimpsonProductions.net

Acknowledgements

I first want to thank my wife, Lisa. Without her, this book would never have happened. Thank you for believing in me and for your willingness to go on this journey together. I am grateful that God has put us together and I am so thankful for our wonderful family, who I know would not be possible without all of your hard work and dedication. Your love for the Lord is truly inspiring and challenges me daily.

I also wish to thank Pastor Sharon Daugherty and her husband, the late Pastor Billy Joe Daugherty. You imparted so much into Lisa and me over the years. You both believed in us when very few did. Thank you so much.

TABLE OF CONTENTS

Introduction 9

Chapter 1 My Journey 13

Chapter 2 God's Standard for Our Lives 23

Chapter 3 The Fear of the Lord Produces Holiness 37

Chapter 4 Change Your Mind —
   Allowing God's Word to Change You 51

Chapter 5 Prayer Changes Things 67

Chapter 6 Accountability — Why and What is it? 77

Chapter 7 Game Plan for Practical Steps 91

Chapter 8 Help for Parents 101

Chapter 9 Help for Wives: a word from Lisa Goforth 109

A Word From The Author 125

About the Author 127

Scriptures to Help You 129

Resources 133

Bibliography 135

INTRODUCTION

"Don't copy the behavior and customs of this world, but let God transform you into a new person by changing the way you think…"

Romans 12:2

The urgency in my heart to write this book has grown stronger and stronger by the day. My life has been changed and now I want to help others. After meeting with men for the past sixteen years I have seen what an addiction to pornography can do. I have seen too many people who are unprepared to step into eternity. A large group of people are living a double life and have allowed sexual sin to dominate their lives.

Jesus in Matthew 7:21-23 warns us, "Not everyone who calls out to me, 'Lord! Lord!' will enter the Kingdom of Heaven. Only those who actually do the will of my Father in heaven will enter. On judgment day many will say to me, 'Lord! Lord! We prophesied in your name and cast out demons in your name and performed many miracles in your name.' But I will reply, 'I never knew you. Get away from me, you who break God's laws.'" These are people who call him Lord, yet they will not be ready for what is about to come. There are different reasons why they are not ready. This life is a test and what we do with this short amount of time determines where we spend eternity.

God hates sexual sin and so should we. We cannot allow it in our lives if we are going to fulfill God's plan for us. I realize this may go against what some are teaching today, but we need to be aware of what the whole Bible says. After reading through the entire Bible many times, I have come to believe that many will not be ready for Christ's return. The Bible warns us over and over again about this, but too many are trying to justify their lifestyles. I know, because I was this way for many years.

How many marriages have been destroyed, and how many dreams have been aborted due to sexual immorality? Proverbs 7:26-27 explains it this way, "For she has been the ruin of many; many men have been her victims. Her house is the road to the grave. Her bedroom is the den of death." An untold number of Christian leaders are being taken out by sexual immorality which affects their lives and numerous others.

Because I have shared my testimony about getting free from my pornography and alcohol addictions, people contact me on a regular basis asking for help. There are too many people for me to be able to help them all. This book is a way to help reach more people. If you called and asked me to meet with you, the message in this book is exactly what I would tell you in person. The principles and practical steps are what I have learned over the last sixteen years by meeting with men of all ages and from all walks of life. It is also what I have learned through my personal struggle with a pornography addiction that almost destroyed my life and marriage.

Sin always takes you further than you think you would go. According to the website Covenant Eyes, nine out of ten boys are exposed to porn before the age of eighteen[1], 68% of young adult men and 18% of women use porn at least once every week[2], and 64% of Christian men and 15% of Christian women say that they watch porn at least once a month.[3] You can see by these statistics that most of us at some point have dealt with pornography or sexually immoral thoughts. This life is a test. We all face temptation but it's how we handle it that matters. If you don't deal with sexual immorality it can affect what you do in this life and the one to come. The battle is real, but the battle is winnable.

> *"The temptations in your life are no different from what others experience. And God is faithful. He will not allow the temptation to be more than you can*

stand. When you are tempted, he will show you a way out so that you can endure."

1 Corinthians 10:13

Chapter 1

My Journey

My story started when I was eight years old. I remember being invited to my friend's house to play. While we were in his garage, we found a box. My heart raced as I opened the box. Inside was a stack of pornographic magazines. I remember feeling guilty, but at the same time excited. When that box came open, it also opened the door to my addiction.

By the time I got to high school I began to hunt for this stuff just like a drug addict. We would pay people to buy it for us or we would steal it from other friends. The internet was starting to come around when I was in college and it made it a whole lot easier to get ahold of porn. I put on this front by acting like everything was great. I didn't want anyone to find out that I was addicted to pornography. I remember going to the altar during chapel at school and repenting, "God, I am sorry." I cried out wanting to see change. One time I was coming back from a short-term mission's trip to Honduras where hundreds of people were saved and healed. Our team stopped in Miami for a couple days of debriefing before flying home. In my hotel room an image caught my eye on the television, and I ended up blowing it. I felt sick inside. How could I do this after being used by God all summer? I wanted to share with someone about my addiction because I wanted to be free, but I was afraid. What if I was the only one that was going through this? Guilt consumed me. I thought I was weird. I believed in God, but my Christian walk was like a roller coaster ride.

When I got married, I thought sex would satisfy that desire. In reality, it only made it worse. Sex did not satisfy. I was confused by this, but eventually realized that lust can never be satisfied. The images that I had looked at all those years and the habitual masturbation had affected my body and mind. My wife would be in the other room and I would be on the computer. I could hear her coming and it was all I could do to clear the computer fast enough before she got into the room. I thought if she found out she would leave me. I hated what I had become and was very discouraged at this point in my life. I felt like this addiction was my master, and I was its slave. It was as if it led me around with a chain around my neck.

I had come to the point in my life where I turned my back on God. I even said, "God, I can't continue on like this. I'm done." Alcohol became a way of escape for me. It was a way for me to cope with the pain that I was dealing with. The alcohol, along with the pornography, had created a very volatile environment within our family. I kept thinking to myself, "What if I died? What if I die and they find out who I really am?" I was a fake. I was addicted, but I wanted to stop. However, I couldn't seem to get past the addictions.

I was tired—tired of dealing with it and I wanted out.

My mother and father-in-law would often give me Christian books that I honestly did not read. They ended up in a stack on our mantle, until one day a certain book caught my attention. It was by John Bevere called *A Heart of Blaze*. This book stirred a hunger in me to once and for all be free from my addiction.

Not too long after that, a defining moment happened in my life while on a business trip to New Orleans. I finally had enough. After drinking all night and shutting the bars down, I was drunk and I didn't know how to get back to my hotel. When I finally made it back to the hotel room early in the morning, I cried out to God while I was still drunk. He met me in that room. I was amazed. I couldn't understand how or why He would still love me after all that I had done. I had reached my end and knew it was time to get help.

It's when we have to come to our end, that healing can begin. Have you been caught or are you really ready to ask God to forgive you and stop what you are doing? I often wonder what would have happened to me that night if I would have died.

I came back home and talked with my wife. We had many talks during this time about my addiction. It was painful at times, but I felt it was necessary for her to know what I was going through. I had lived a double life for many years and wanted her to know so I could be transparent with her, but also so she could help me. We had grown apart over the years, so we needed to have our relationship restored. With the porn addiction had also come an addiction to alcohol. This caused me to not be around my family on the weekends and we sometimes had separate vacations. I was either at the bar, out playing golf and getting drunk, or hanging out with my guy friends. Alcohol seemed to mask my pain for a short time, but reality would set back in when I sobered up. I decided during this period to stop drinking. I knew if I was to beat this porn addiction, alcohol would not help. I had done many stupid things while drinking.

This was a personal choice I have made to avoid alcohol. It was necessary for me as I could never have just one drink. I would always get drunk. My personality tends to be the type that when I am doing something then I am ALL in. When it's a good habit it's a good thing, but when it's destructive then it's not so good.

This began a long process of restoration in my life. We went back to church, and I also enrolled in a discipleship course at my church. In that class, I was able share openly what I had done and the healing process began. With God and the help of other men in my life, I began my journey to freedom! It did not happen overnight. It was a long process of staying in the Word of God and remaining accountable to other men. Now, I can truly say I am free today.

I tried it without God for so many years, and it did not work. If you want to get free and stay free, you must turn your life over to Jesus Christ. You may be thinking to yourself I did turn my life over, but I still struggle. But the struggle is so much harder without God. We will talk about that later in the book.

After meeting with many men and helping them walk out of their addiction over the past several years, I recognize the importance of sharing what I have learned. I did not set out to be the person that people talk with about their addictions and pains. However, because I was willing to go on television and share my past mistakes, people feel free to open up to me. Through hundreds of conversations, I've learned that most of us are dealing with issues (sins) in our lives that we have tried to keep hidden. People tend to think that they can handle things on their own. By the time most men end up meeting with me, they are in the middle of a personal crisis. Some are heading to prison, heading towards divorce, caught in an affair, or are just simply way off course. Their stories, just like mine, are really all connected.

Many of us live in secrecy with our thought life. We act like everything is okay, but in reality our addiction to pornography controls us. The Bible says, "Guard your heart above all else, for it determines the course of your life" (Proverbs 4:23). The King James Version says to "*keep* your heart …" Keep means to protect, maintain, or obey. Because I did not heed the advice of this verse, I allowed pornography to control my life for many years which altered God's plan for my life.

Surrender Your Life to Christ

The first step to getting your freedom is surrendering your whole life to Jesus Christ. If you are not saved, you need to surrender your life to Jesus Christ. However, you need to count the cost before you make this decision. What does this mean? Too many people go down to the altar at a church service, but don't really count the cost of surrendering their life to Jesus Christ. He is asking for your whole life.

It is your choice. Many start the race, but don't finish because they don't count the cost. Jesus said, "You can enter God's Kingdom only through the narrow gate. The highway to hell is broad, and its gate is wide for the many who choose that way. But the gateway to life is very narrow and the road is difficult, and only a few ever find it" (Matthew 7:13-14). I really like the way the Amplified Bible says it, ""But the gate is narrow (contracted by pressure) and the way is straitened and compressed that leads away to life, and few are those who find it" (Matthew 7:14 AMP). According to this, the way to heaven is on the road less traveled. It's not always easy or comfortable. Too many don't count the cost before they start the journey. Jesus said, "And he who does not take his cross and follow after Me is not worthy of Me. He who finds his life will lose it, and he who loses his life for My sake will find it" (Matthew 10:38-39 NKJV). It is your choice whether or not to surrender your whole life.

Don't take it lightly. He is asking for your whole life. Are you willing to give it? In return, you receive eternity in heaven and true freedom. Think carefully about your decision. He is asking for *ALL* of you.

How do you give all of your life to Jesus? You confess Jesus Christ as your Lord and Savior and completely turn your life over to him. The Bible says, "For with the heart one believes unto righteousness, and with the mouth confession is made unto salvation" (Romans 10:10 NKJV). Pray this prayer if you have counted the cost and desire to make Jesus the Lord and Savior of your life: "God, please forgive me of my sins. Jesus, I turn my whole life over to you. I confess you as Lord and Savior of my life. I choose from this day forward to serve you with all my heart. I thank you that you have forgiven me from all my sins."

If you prayed that prayer, then welcome to the family of God. Find a local church and tell them about the decision you just made. Get connected with that church and let them know what you are walking out. Now let's begin your journey to freedom together.

My Journey

"And you will know the truth, and the truth will set you free."

—John 8:32

Chapter 2

God's Standard for Our Lives

God has a standard for your life in the area of sexual morality. His standard is that we do not allow any immorality into our lives. So what does that mean?

For the purposes of this book, sexual immorality is defined as fornication (sex outside of marriage), adultery (sex with some other than your spouse), homosexuality (sex with the same gender), unlawful lust (looking at porn), and licentiousness (sexually unrestrained and going beyond the customary or proper bounds or rules). Ephesians 5:3 says, "Let there be no sexual immorality, impurity, or greed among you. Such sins have no place among God's people." One translation from this verse says "..not even a hint."[4]

A hint is defined as a very slight or hardly noticeable amount.[5] That means we should not allow any sexual immorality in our thoughts or our lives. God has a high standard of living for us. The world says we can live however we want and have absolute freedom. When people live outside of God's standard, they are slaves to sin. They are not free. There are even Christians today who have changed what they believe because of secular pressure. However, our standard must come from the Word of God. In Galatians 5:19-21, the apostle Paul warns, "When you follow the desires of your sinful nature, the results are very clear: sexual immorality, impurity, and lustful pleasures. As I have before, that anyone living that sort of life will not inherit the kingdom of God." This can seem harsh, but God loves us and wants the best for our lives. He knows that if we continue living in sexual immorality we cannot live the life He has called us to live. The Bible goes on to say, "Just because something is technically legal doesn't mean that it's spiritually appropriate. If I went around doing whatever I thought I could get by with, I'd be a slave to my whims" (1 Corinthians 6:12 MSG). A small crack in a dam may not seem like a big deal compared to its immense size, but over time it can have devastating effects. Everyday pressure causes the crack to widen and weakens the dam. The same can be true in our own lives. Small cracks can cause big problems when left unchecked. The pressures of life push our flesh to do something to relieve that pressure and if we have not purified our thought lives, then we can easily fall into temptation. You many think that what you are doing is not a big deal, but remember the Bible says: "even a hint" of sexual immorality is destructive.

When we allow sin to dominate our lives we end up having to continually tell lies. This can set a pattern in our lives for being dishonest in other areas. Jesus tells us, "If you are faithful in little things, you will be faithful in large ones. But if you are dishonest in little things, you won't be honest with greater responsibilities" (Luke 16:10). Dishonesty is a character issue that affects other areas of our lives. We spend so much of our time covering up our sin that we end up lying on a regular basis.

I remember when I was deeply entrenched in my own porn addiction. I was not just lying about my addiction but other matters as well. It really led me to lead a double life. There is so much pressure in the lies and dishonesty associated with sexual immorality. What if someone finds out what we are really like? The image we have tried so hard to portray, in reality, is not even the truth. The longer we continue to live in sexual immorality, the more deception takes place in our lives. If this is not dealt with, it will eventually affect not only our destiny during this life but where and how we spend eternity. I will never forget the day I came clean and finally told someone what was going on in my life. It was so freeing.

Sin should not dominate us

Once we have made Jesus Christ our Lord and savior, sin should not dominate our lives anymore. To better understand this, we need to look at Romans 6, "For we know that our old self was crucified with him so that the body ruled by sin might be done away with, that we should no longer be slaves to sin …" (Romans 6:6 NIV). Throughout the whole chapter of Romans 6, it repeats that sin should not have dominion over us anymore. The New Living Translation says, "Do not let sin control the way you live; do not give in to sinful desires. Do not let any part of your body become an instrument of evil to serve sin. Instead, give yourselves completely to God, for you were dead, but now you have new life. So use your whole body as an instrument to do what is right for the glory of God" (Romans 6:12-14). Sin should not control us. This fact did not become a reality in my life until I read this passage numerous times and spoke it out loud over and over. I remember the day I realized that sin should not dominate my life anymore. I got so excited because I realized at that point I was already free. We have been given authority over the devil. We can allow sexual immorality to dominate our lives or we can refuse to be dominated by sin because of what Christ has done for us. "In this way, He disarmed the spiritual rulers and authorities. He shamed them publicly by His victory over them on the cross" (Colossians 2:15). The bottom line is that Jesus already defeated the devil. The battle is in our thought life. Sin dominates us because we don't realize that Jesus already died so that we can be free from sin and immorality.

I used to think it was impossible to live a sexually pure life and I have heard many others say the same thing. According to the Bible, it is possible. The Bible says, "No temptation has overtaken you except such as is common to man; but God is faithful, who will not allow you to be tempted beyond what you are able, but with the temptation will also make the way of escape, that you may be able to bear it" (1 Corinthians 10:12-13 NKJV). This is great news because God promises that He will not allow you to be tempted beyond what you are able to resist. God is not a liar. He is faithful to His word and He gives us the ability to walk out a pure thought life. It is possible, but the choice is ultimately up to us. We have to realize that Jesus lives within us and that he died on the cross for every one of our sins.

"[God] disarmed the principalities and powers that were ranged against us and made a bold display and public example of them, in triumphing over them in Him and in it [the cross]" (Colossians 2:15 AMP).

OUR BODIES AND FLEEING TEMPTATION

Our bodies are the temple of the Holy Spirit. When we really think about it in this context, it makes us realize how important our bodies are. Think about the fact that God's spirit resides in us and that He is always with us. "Don't you realize that your body is the temple of the Holy Spirit, who lives in you and was given to you by God? You do not belong to yourself" (1 Corinthians 6:19). The word temple means a place to dwell, a shrine, or a sacred place. If we can understand this it will help us when we are tempted with sexual immorality. We must honor God with our bodies. 1 Thessalonians 4:3-4 says, "God's will is for you to be holy, so stay away from all sexual sin. Then each of you will control their own body and live in holiness and honor." Masturbation, homosexuality, pre-marital sex, and adultery are not holy and honorable according to the Bible. People often ask me if masturbation is okay. My personal answer is no. What are you thinking on while doing this? I realize some may be shocked by me bringing this up, but it needs to be addressed. Lust is never satisfied and it always takes you further than you think you would go. You can always find someone who will help justify your addiction, but I look to the Bible to define the standard of conduct for my life. One of the problems caused by masturbation is difficulty with intimacy in your marriage because your body is used to the act of masturbation. Many men think once they get married they won't have to deal with masturbation anymore, but that is far from the truth. Lust is never satisfied. God made sex and it is good and pleasing to Him within the confines of marriage between a man and a women.

Guarding and protecting what we look at is part of honoring God with our bodies. Jesus says, "But I say, anyone who even looks at a woman with lust has already committed adultery with her in his heart" (Matthew 5:28). This verse very clearly defines sexual immorality. It said that if you even *look* lustfully at a woman you have committed adultery. Wow! What we look at matters. What we do with our eyes matters. What we look at will determine what we think about and eventually what we do. David got himself into trouble because of what he looked at. 2 Samuel 11:1-5 (NKJV) tells the story,

"It happened in the spring of the year, at the time when kings go out to battle, that David sent Joab and his servants with him, and all Israel; and they destroyed the people of Ammon and besieged Rabbah. But David remained at Jerusalem. Then it happened one evening that David arose from his bed and walked on the roof of the king's house. And from the roof he saw a woman bathing, and the woman was very beautiful to behold. So David sent and inquired about the woman. And someone said, "Is this not Bathsheba, the daughter of Eliam, the wife of Uriah the Hittite?" Then David sent messengers, and took her; and she came to him, and he lay with her, for she was cleansed from her impurity; and she returned to her house. And the woman conceived; so she sent and told David, and said, "I am with child.""

Verse 2 says "from the roof he saw a woman bathing…" David was really at the wrong place at the wrong time. After reading this passage, we see his first mistake was that he should have been at the battle with his troops. His second mistake was not looking away when he saw Bathsheba bathing. You can read the rest of the story, but it cost David dearly. What we look at has a huge impact on us. David's story is like many of us—we can simply end up at the wrong place at the wrong time. There are also times that we put ourselves in compromising situations that can challenge our integrity. If David's story was written today, it would read something like this: While David could not sleep late at night he got up and turned on the television. While watching, an immoral image came across the screen and he did not look away. How many of us can relate to this story verses the actual story from the Bible? What we look at matters! Psalm 119:37 says, "Turn away my eyes from looking at worthless things…" It is our choice what we look at. There are things we just do not need to see. I have trained myself over the years to turn away from things that would cause me to fall into lust. Sometimes I have to look away when I see a person dressed inappropriately or sometimes when I am watching a movie. In both situations, I have taught myself to turn away or walk out of a movie if need be. The Bible says, "Flee from sexual immorality…" (1 Corinthians 6:18 NIV). The word flee means to run away, shun or escape. Whether it is leaving a movie you should not be watching, or not being with a woman in an inappropriate place or situation, escaping immorality is the best course of action.

Now let's look at a great story from the Bible about someone who had to escape sexual immorality. Here is Joseph's story:

"Now Joseph was handsome in form and appearance. And it came to pass after these things that his master's wife cast longing eyes on Joseph, and she said, 'Lie with me.' But he refused and said to his master's wife, 'Look, my master does not know what *is* with me in the house, and he has committed all that he has to my hand. There is no one greater in this house than I, nor has he kept back anything from me but you, because you are his wife. How then can I do this great wickedness, and sin against God?'

So it was, as she spoke to Joseph day by day, that he did not heed her, to lie with her *or* to be with her. But it happened about this time, when Joseph went into the house to do his work, and none of the men of the house was inside, that she caught him by his garment, saying, 'Lie with me.' But he left his garment in her hand, and fled and ran outside" (Genesis 39:6b-12 NKJV).

This story is amazing to me, because in verse 10 she tried to seduce him not just once, but day after day. The devil is relentless. He comes at us over and over again. The best course of action is to remove ourselves from compromising situations. Joseph could have given in to his flesh and compromised, but he stayed faithful. His decision to flee had a ripple effect. Little did he know that his decision would set into motion events that would cause him to become Pharaoh's right hand man. His position allowed him to save Egypt and his family from famine. Decisions made today affect not only what happens to us now, but it affects others in the future. If not dealt with, our sins can ruin us and negatively impact those we love.

A lustful appetite is never satisfied. What we feed on is what we crave. The more we look at immoral images the more we want to take them in. The apostle Peter says, "They commit adultery with their eyes, and their desire for sin is never satisfied" (2 Peter 2:14). It becomes a challenge to have a pure thought life when we are constantly filling ourselves with junk. This is why it is important to guard what we look at and what we watch. You will always have issues with sexual immorality if you choose to keep watching immoral things. I know some would say this is legalism, but it has been a key to maintaining my freedom.

A Call to Action:

What weight or sin is trying to hold you back? This is the part that can be hard, but seek God and be willing to admit where you need help. We must realize we need God. The bottom line is we cannot do it without him. John 15:5 says, "For apart from me you can do nothing." What area in your life do you need to ask God to forgive you? Pray this prayer as we begin: "God I am asking for a change to take place in my thought life. I realize I need help and I am asking you now to help me. Forgive me for allowing this addiction to stay in my life. I choose from this day forward to give you my whole body. Thank you for helping me walk this out." This is a journey that takes time. The key is to not give up or quit in the process. You will discover practical steps that will help you walk out your freedom. It did not happen for me overnight. I had to remain steadfast and wholly committed.

Practical step:

Small steps are the key to making big changes. We will be talking about what small steps you can take in your life that can help in your quest for freedom. First, get sleep! This sounds basic but in order to live a disciplined life in all areas we need our rest. Lack of sleep will result in making bad decisions and it is hard to fight when you don't feel like it. So turn the TV off or get off the internet a little early and go to sleep in order to get up refreshed. This step helped me tremendously in my journey.

Discussion Questions:

1) In your own words, how do you describe God's standard? _____
_____
_____
_____
_____
_____

2) After reading this chapter, are there any areas you have allowed sin to dominate your thought life? If so, what areas? _____
_____
_____
_____
_____
_____

3) What is one way you can guard your eyes? _____
_____
_____
_____
_____
_____

Chapter 3

THE FEAR OF THE LORD PRODUCES HOLINESS

"When men no longer fear God, they transgress his laws without hesitation."[6]
—*A.W. Tozer*

In 2 Chronicles 26, we meet King Uzziah who was crowned King of Judah at the age of sixteen. He was a young king who knew he needed the Lord's help. "Uzziah sought God during the days of Zechariah, who taught him to fear God. And as long as the king sought guidance from the Lord, God gave him success" (2 Chronicles 26:5).

Uzziah went on to defeat all his enemies, build fortified towers, construct forts, and cultivated great herds of livestock. He assembled an army of well-trained warriors and had advanced weapons of war designed by experts. By all accounts, he was a success and his fame became well known. In verse 16 we read, "But when he had become powerful, he also became proud, which led to his downfall. He sinned against the Lord his God by entering the sanctuary of the Lord's temple and personally burning incense on the incense altar."

The priests urged him to stop since it was not the work of the king to burn incense, but the king raged against the priests. As he stood there, leprosy suddenly broke out on his forehead. "So King Uzziah had leprosy until the day he died. He lived in isolation in a separate house, for he was excluded from the Temple of the Lord" (2 Chronicles 26:21). This is a tragic ending to a king who was taught to fear God. What happened, and where did the king go wrong?

King Uzziah lost his fear of the Lord. I truly believe that this is why so many struggle with sin. They have no fear of the Lord. The fear of the Lord is true wisdom. The Amplified Bible says, "The reverent and worshipful fear of the Lord is the beginning and the principal and choice part of knowledge [its starting point and its essence]; but fools despise skillful and godly Wisdom, instruction, and discipline" (Proverbs 1:7 AMP). So according to the book of

Proverbs the starting point of godly wisdom is the fear of the Lord.

What exactly is the fear of the Lord? The fear of the Lord is the awe, reverence, and respect toward God. W.E. Vines goes on to define it as "a wholesome dread of displeasing Him."[7] This may seem heavy but we must come to a biblical understanding of what the fear of the Lord is in order to really know God. When we fear the Lord, we hate sin and want obey Him no matter the outcome. I look at the fear of the Lord as a guard for us. It makes us think about the decision we are about to make. Without the fear of the Lord, we see no need to repent and change our lifestyle. Who you fear is who you will obey. It gives us boldness to obey God rather than man. It pushes us to not sin.

The fear of the Lord is the starting point for godly wisdom. "Fear of the Lord is the foundation of true knowledge, but fools despise wisdom and discipline" (Proverbs 1:7). When my family built our first home in Oklahoma, we found out the importance of the house's foundation. It is the solid, concrete slab upon which the whole house rests. If the foundation isn't stable then later on cracks can develop in the slab and in the walls. The same is true when the fear of the Lord is your foundation for your personal relationship with God. Without a proper understanding and the fear of the Lord in your life, cracks can form in this foundation. A cracked foundation will eventually cause the whole house to break and fall apart. I allowed a crack in my life and it opened the door to pornography, alcohol addiction, and a total lack of self-control.

The fear of the Lord is something we have to actively seek out. I love the way Proverbs talks about it, "My child, listen to what I say, and treasure my commands. Tune your ears to wisdom, and concentrate on understanding. Cry out for insight, and ask for understanding. Search for them as you would for silver; seek them like hidden treasures. Then you will understand what it means to fear the Lord, and you will gain knowledge of God" (Proverbs 2:1-5). This passage talks about seeking the fear of the Lord as one would seek for treasure. How much effort would you use if you knew that there was a treasure hidden on your property? How much time would you spend looking for it? How much more valuable is the fear of the Lord in our lives than earthly treasure? When we truly value something we will take the time to seek it out. By seeking wisdom we find the fear of the Lord. I began to seek out the fear of the Lord throughout the Bible and began to see that the fear of the Lord was imperative. Psalms goes as far to say that, "The secret of the Lord is with those who fear Him" (Psalms 25:14 NKJV). This was truly life changing for me.

Let's look at an example of what can happen if the fear of the Lord is not the foundation in our lives. In I Samuel 10-12, Saul is crowned the first King of Israel. Saul was chosen by God to be their king. God told the Israelites through the prophet Samuel, "If you fear the Lord and serve Him and obey His voice, and do not rebel against the commandment of the Lord, then both you and the king who reigns over you will continue following the Lord your God. However, if you do not obey the voice of the Lord, but rebel against the commandment of the Lord, then the hand of the Lord will be against you" (1 Samuel 12:14-15 NKJV). As the story unfolded, we see that Saul did not continue in the fear of the Lord as Samuel had warned him. "So he demanded,

'Bring me the burnt offering and the peace offerings!' And Saul sacrificed the burnt offering himself. Just as Saul was finishing with the burnt offering, Samuel arrived. Saul went out to meet and welcome him, but Samuel said, 'What is this you have done?' Saul replied, 'I saw my men scattering from me, and you didn't arrive when you said you would, and the Philistines are at Micmash ready for battle. So I said, "The Philistines are ready to march against us at Gilgal, and I haven't even asked for the Lord's help!" So I felt compelled to offer the burnt offering myself before you came.' 'How foolish!' Samuel exclaimed. 'You have not kept the command the Lord your God gave you. Had you kept it, the Lord would have established your kingdom over Israel forever. But now your kingdom must end, for the Lord has sought out a man after his own heart. The Lord has already appointed him to be the leader of his people, because you have not kept the Lord's command'" (1 Samuel 13:9-14 NLT).

Saul disobeyed God by sacrificing the burnt offering which was not his to sacrifice. Because of the pressure of the people, Saul decided not to wait on Samuel, but instead performed the sacrifice himself. We will obey who we fear, and Saul feared the people more than he did God.

As the story continues, Saul was told by God to destroy all the people from Amalek and to spare no one. In I Samuel 15:9 it says "Saul and his men spared Agag's life and kept the best of the sheep and goats, the cattle, the fat calves, and the lambs—everything, in fact, that appealed to them. They destroyed only what was worthless or of poor quality." The Lord said to Samuel that He greatly regretted setting up Saul as king because he did not follow His commandments. Saul told Samuel that he had obeyed God, but Samuel showed Saul how disobedient his actions were. "To obey is better than sacrifice …and rebellion is as the sin of witchcraft" (1 Samuel 15:22-23 NKJV).

Saul thought that because he had obeyed most of God's commands that he was safe. But partial obedience is still sin. Partial obedience is rebellion and rebellion leads to death. This story shows the importance of dealing with sin in our own lives. Saul thought he was obeying God by partial obedience, but God was not pleased with his rebellion.

Is it possible our lives at times do not please God? I feel the answer is yes. We have the ability to please God by our conduct. Saul was chosen for leadership, but because of his rebellion he was taken out of that position. If we don't deal with sexual immorality in our lives then the same can happen to us. People have aborted the call of God on their lives due to sexual immorality. It is imperative that we deal with all sexual impurity in our lives. As we talked about before, we should not have "even a hint" of sexual immorality. If you have messed up, God is faithful and just to forgive us of our sins when we repent and His grace gives us the ability to walk it out.

Holiness

"Holiness comes as a result of the fear of God."[8]
— Pastor Billy Joe Daugherty

Once the fear of the Lord is evident in our lives, we begin the process of developing holiness. Holiness is, fundamentally, cutting off or separation from what is unclean, and consecration to what is pure.[9] The process of holiness has been misunderstood by many Christians today. Many attribute it to legalism which is so far from the truth. Holiness is a characteristic of God and is talked about throughout the Bible. In fact, the Bible says "Pursue peace with all people, and holiness, without which no one will see the Lord" (Hebrews 12:14 NKJV). If this is true, then holiness needs to be evident in our lives. The Amplified version of this verse says to *pursue holiness*. This is something we have to seek after. The more I seek holiness the closer I feel to God and the more sin does not seem as attractive as it used to. It keeps me more focused on eternity and what is about to come rather than on a short term pleasure and instant gratification.

If you truly want to be free from sin then you must study holiness and receive it in your life. The Bible says, "But now since you have been set free from sin and have become [willing] slaves to God, you have your benefit, resulting in sanctification [being made holy and set apart for God's purpose], and the outcome [of this] is eternal life" (Romans 6:22 AMP). The reward of holiness is eternal life!

This is such a powerful passage on how important holiness is in our lives.

So What is the Big Deal?

As Christians we are called to be holy in everything we do. Our actions during our short time on this earth matter. The Living Bible says, "Obey God because you are his children; don't slip back into your old ways—doing evil because you knew no better. But be holy now in everything you do, just as the Lord is holy, who invited you to be his child. He himself has said, 'You must be holy, for I am holy'" (1 Peter 1:14-16 TLB). Where and how we spend eternity depends on what we do during our short amount of time on earth. Many people do not like hearing this, but you are not rejecting my opinion by not believing. You are rejecting God's Word. In this passage we are told to be holy because God our Father is holy, and we are to be like Him. This is a command from God and not just a suggestion.

I always felt restrained by my Christian beliefs before I truly surrendered my life to Jesus. If you asked me while I was bound by pornography I would have said God loves me and He knows my weaknesses. We tend to make excuses for our sins, but we must realize there is a price to pay for allowing sin to stay in our lives. Sin separates us from God and keeps us from doing what He has called us to do. God calls us to be holy just as He is holy.

Now, let's read it out of the New Living Translation. "So prepare your minds for action and exercise self-control. Put all your hope in the gracious salvation that will come to you when Jesus Christ is revealed to the world" (1 Peter 1:13). The Bible would not tell us to be self-controlled if it was impossible. That means we are to self-controlled is: the ability to exercise restraint or control over one's feelings, emotions, reactions, etc.[10] With God in us we have the ability to be self-controlled. We cannot expect to be watching movies with immoral images and remain holy in our thoughts and actions. Freedom does not mean doing whatever we want to. This is what the world says freedom is but ultimately this turns into bondage.

Sanctification

People ask me how to practically walk out holiness, and I would say that it is through the work of sanctification. I know many of us can get lost in big theological words. I feel it is important to know these terms and take the time to define them. The definition of sanctification is: "A process or the state of proper functioning. To sanctify someone or something is to set that person or thing apart for the use intended by its designer. A pen is 'sanctified' when used to write. Eyeglasses are 'sanctified' when used to improve sight. In the theological sense, things are 'sanctified' when they are used for the purpose God intends. A human being is sanctified, therefore, when he or she lives according to God's design and purpose."[11]

It is further defined as being "sanctified or holy. God's people are to progressively grow in holiness until the Day of the Lord, at which point all believers will be completely sanctified."[12] When Jesus died and rose again, He defeated the devil and it was a finished work, but we have to make the decision to walk out that freedom. That is where sanctification comes in. The sanctification process can be equated to how a crucible works. Precious metals are poured into a container called a crucible that can withstand high temperatures. The crucible is heated and the impurities come to the surface. The metal worker skims the impurities off the top and continues with the heating process until all the impurities are removed from the metal. Sanctification is the same process. In this life there will be tests and temptations. These represent our personal time in the crucible. When impurities come to the surface in our lives, are we going to allow God to remove those? That is the act of sanctification. Unforgiveness, anger, submission to authority, and sexual immorality are just a few of the areas that we need to allow the sanctification process take place. When heat or pressure is applied, what is on the inside will come out. I personally have to choose on a regular basis with what I allow myself to view. Tempting thoughts may come, but we have to make a choice to be separate from the things of this world. Reading the Word of God, memorizing scripture, and renewing your mind are the keys to walking out the fear of the Lord and sanctification.

A Call to Action:

Setbacks can happen in the process. What you do if you experience a setback is what separates the men from the boys. Too many give up when they mess up. They let condemnation keep them from asking God for forgiveness and being transparent with those around them.

Practical Step:

One practical step I have taken over the years that helps me not fall back into immorality is to be intentional about what I watch on TV or in a movie. What we feed on will affect our thought life. When I watch a movie, the remote control is beside me. If something comes on the screen that I know will lead me down a path I don't want to go, I fast forward or shut it off. You can look at these practical steps as legalism or steps to help you not slip back into bondage and immorality.

<u>Discussion Questions:</u>

1) How do you describe the fear of the Lord?

_____
_____
_____
_____
_____
_____

2) Explain the sanctification process? What does it look like in our lives? _____

_____
_____
_____
_____
_____
_____

Chapter 4

CHANGE YOUR MIND — ALLOWING GOD'S WORD TO CHANGE YOU

"You can make a decision to be a champion if you want to be, it will cost you something. It will cost you the price of renewing your mind so your thinking is right through reading the word, hearing the Word, meditating on the Word, and speaking the Word."[13]
- *Pastor Billy Joe Daugherty*

The phrase, "renewing your mind" means simply allowing God's Word to change the way we think. We have to realize that each of us are three-part beings. We are spirits, we have souls, and we live in bodies. The soul is made up of the mind, will, and emotions. The only way to change the way we think and not be controlled by our emotions or our flesh is by consistently renewing our minds with the Word of God. When a person gets saved, their spirit man is renewed, but their mind still needs to be transformed. Romans 12:2 (NKJV) "And do not be conformed to this world, but be transformed by the renewing of your mind, that you may prove what is that good and acceptable and perfect will of God." Our spirit man should dominate us rather than our souls or flesh. When we do not spend daily time renewing our minds, then our flesh controls our actions. I am reminded of a young man I met years ago who was in a missionary family. Although he had confessed Jesus as his personal savior, a pornography addiction still gripped his thought life. He told that me that there was no way he could ever be free. His flesh was ruling his life because he had never taken the time to renew his mind with the Word of God and allow it to change his thoughts. This is the same way that a pastor can get up on a Sunday morning and preach to his congregation, yet he is simultaneously living in an immoral relationship. Both of these examples happened because of a lack of control in their thought lives. Just because we go to the altar and confess during a service or just because our title is a minster, does not mean that we should stop reading God's Word. We can seek deliverance or help from others, but ultimately we have to spend time renewing our mind. To explain it practically, we can equate renewing our mind to programming a computer. The computer is fed information and the actions we perform are the results of how our mind is programmed. If we feed our mind with pornography, it is no surprise that we would have an addiction. In order to gain freedom, we must stop feeding our mind with ungodly images and choose to fix our mind on those things that are true, honest, just, pure, lovely and of a good report.[14] "And now, brothers, as I close this letter, let me say this one more thing: Fix your thoughts on what is true and good and right. Think about things that are pure and lovely, and dwell on the fine, good things in others. Think about all you can praise God for and be glad about" (Philippians 4:8 Living Bible TLB).

Just because a thought comes into your mind doesn't mean you have to dwell on it, nor does it mean we have sinned. This is where many people get into trouble. Not every thought that comes into your mind is your thought. The devil will try to bring a thought into our mind and try to tempt us. If it's not godly, then we must simply choose not to think on it and replace that thought with the Word of God. The Bible says, "...and we lead every thought and purpose away captive into the obedience of Christ the Messiah, the Anointed One ..." (2 Corinthians 10:5

AMPC). The key is to deal with the thought and get rid of it as soon as it comes.

We can renew our mind by hearing the Word, reading the Word, seeking the Word, meditating on the Word, and speaking the Word. In this chapter we will go into each area and give practical insights on how to apply these principles to our life.

Hearing the Word

The first way to renew our mind is to hear the Word. Romans 10:17 says, "So faith comes from hearing, that is, hearing the Good News about Christ." A great way to hear the Word is to attend a local church that preaches the Bible. I cannot say enough good things about my local church and how much I have grown spiritually by sitting under my pastor's teaching. There are many great churches. Visit several churches and pray about which one God wants you to belong. It is critical to find a local church and plant yourself there. What I mean by this is do not just go to church, but get involved. Beyond a Sunday or Wednesday service, you can listen to the Word on podcasts, YouTube, and CD's. We have a CD that is available on iTunes that you can download that is called *Renew Change Your Mind* that you can listen to throughout your day. I have listened to certain messages over and over again that have really helped me grow in my walk with God and have helped me in my struggles with sexual immorality. The Bible app from Life Church allows you to read the Bible in many different translations and we also have the option to listen to the Bible. Modern technology gives us many options to hear the Word. The Bible describes it as the washing of the Word: "that He might sanctify and cleanse her [the church] with the washing of water by the word" (Ephesians 5:26 NKJV). Let the Word of God wash you while you listen to it. However, while listening is important, it is even more important to obey the Word of God.

READING THE BIBLE

It's critical once we accept Jesus Christ as our personal savior to spend consistent time reading the Bible. 1 Peter 2:2 (NKJV) "as newborn babes, desire the pure milk of the word, that you may grow thereby." A great way to read your Bible daily is the *One Year Bible*. It breaks up the Bible each day by having you read passages from the Old Testament, New Testament, a Psalm, and a Proverb. There are also many free Bible reading plans online that help you know what to read every day. Start by reading a chapter or two each day.

As I read the *One Year Bible* through several times and read one chapter each day in Psalm and Proverbs, I grew to love Psalm and Proverbs. Remember to keep a notebook with you and write down any verses that stand out to you. I have done this for years and have personally found it has helped me remember what God is speaking to me in those verses.

My goal each morning is to spend time with God while reading the Bible and reading over the scriptures I have written down. If you oversleep, then read at lunch or before you go to bed. The bottom line is to make a decision each day to spend time seeking God. Block out time in your day where you can get alone with God. Put in on your calendar if that will help you remember to do it.

If you have a family, you may have to get creative. I've literally had my time with God in a park sitting in my car or even in my garage. When our kids were little it was tough to fit it all in, but I determined to make my time with God a priority. All seasons in life are busy, and if you wait until you're not busy, it's never going to happen. Some seasons are harder than others to make the time.

To be honest there have been times over the years that I did not feel like reading my Bible. It happens to us all. If you miss a few days then just jump right back in and keep seeking after God. The more you spend time seeking God the more you will crave it. When you become hungry for the things of God you will find the time to sit in His presence. We live in a time in history when as Christians we must know what the Bible says for ourselves.

Seeking

The difference for me came when I began to seek after God's Word like treasure. The Bible says,

"My son, if you will receive my words and treasure up my commandments within you, making your ear attentive to skillful and godly Wisdom and inclining and directing your heart and mind to understanding [applying all your powers to the quest for it]; Yes, if you cry out for insight and raise your voice for understanding, if you seek [Wisdom] as for silver and search for skillful and godly Wisdom as for hidden treasures, then you will understand the reverent and worshipful fear of the Lord and find the knowledge of [our omniscient] God" (Proverbs 2:1-5 AMP).

The word "treasures"[15] in the Strong's Concordance means *a secret storehouse*. There is a secret storehouse in the Word of God if we are willing to seek it out! My whole life has been changed because I took the time to seek God. I truly treasure the times I have sat in my car or in my study with my Bible seeking after God through his Word. Push away the things of this world to make sure you have time to spend with God. With a media filled culture, we have to really make sure we have our priorities straight.

Meditate and Memorizing

According to Webster's Ninth New Collegiate Dictionary the word meditate[16] means to practice or to ponder or imagine; implies a definite focusing of one's thoughts on something so as to understand it deeply. It takes work to get in the Word of God and to meditate on it. There are so many distractions and life gets so busy that it can be difficult to spend time with God. It is going to take a sacrifice of your time. The Bible says, "But his delight is in the law of the Lord,

> *And on His law [His precepts and teachings] he [habitually] meditates day and night. And he will be like a tree firmly planted [and fed] by streams of water, which yields its fruit in its season; its leaf does not wither; and in whatever he does, he prospers [and comes to maturity]" (Psalm 1:2-3 AMP).*

Meditating on the word of God is not something we do and then check off our list in the morning when we are finished. We must continue studying God's word throughout the day. For me, a key has been using 3x5 index cards or my notebook to write out Bible verses. I find scriptures on whatever I am struggling with and write them out and then speak them out loud. I look up key word searches in www.biblegateway.com or use my concordance in the back of the Bible. The searches will give plenty of scriptures to choose from that apply to almost any situation. Pick a couple of verses and write them out. I have memorized so many verses because I wrote them out and then I spoke them out loud. I discovered in the process how effective it is to not only read the Bible, but to incorporate speaking it out loud also. What I found was that scriptures would come to my remembrance that I had been meditating on. My thoughts were beginning to change.

It has been said that we remember:

10 percent of what we READ

20 percent of what we HEAR

30 percent of what we SEE and HEAR

70 percent of what we SAY and WRITE[17]

At the end of the book I will give specific verses to help overcome sexual immorality. The more we meditate and memorize the Word the more we get to know God and walk out freedom in our thought lives.

I did not realize initially, but once I made the decision to overcome the addiction to pornography, I started on a journey that has not stopped. Now, I love spending time in God's Word. Let's look at Joshua 1:8 again. "This Book of the Law shall not depart from your mouth, but you shall meditate in it day and night, that you may observe to do according to all that is written in it. For then you will make your way prosperous, and then you will have good success."[18] Remember, the word meditate means to practice or to ponder or imagine; implies a definite focusing of one's thoughts on something so as to understand it deeply. Meditate also means to murmur, to speak, study, or talk. If you want to be free, then make a decision to read the Bible and to study and meditate on it daily.

The Bible says, "Fix these words of mine in your hearts and minds;" (Deuteronomy 11:18 NIV). This may sound basic, but many of us get busy and stop putting God's Word first in our lives. We fix our eyes on the Bible when we spend time reading it. However, there are also distractions can take our focus away from what is important. It is so easy to start each day checking out social media and what is going on online. A status update can turn into looking at all my 'friends' vacation pics and then an hour has passed. Social media isn't bad in and of itself, but our priorities need to be right. We must choose to memorize verses and meditate on them. This is how we change the way we think. What we think about determines what actions we take and how we feel. The Bible says, "For as he thinks in his heart, so is he" (Proverbs 23:7 NKJV).

Remember that once we get saved, your Spirit is the only part of us that is renewed or changed. All that junk we fed our mind over the years has to be replaced with the Word of God. Our mind is the main arena where the devil tries to attack us. I had to replace those thoughts that I had been thinking for so many years with the Word of God. It did not happen overnight. Speaking the Word of God was one of the ways that I changed my thought life. I read chapter six in Romans over and over again. I did this until one day Romans 6:14 stood out to me. It says that sin no longer has dominion over me; it is no longer my master.

That does not mean there have not been any issues with my thought life since then. The difference is that when a thought comes that is not of God I do what the Bible says: "…and we take captive every thought to make it obedient to Christ" (2 Corinthians 10:5 NIV). Just because I have a bad thought does not mean I have done anything wrong; the problem comes when I continue to dwell on that bad thought. Men often tell me they cannot help their thought life, but that is not true according to the Word of God. Just because a thought comes does not mean we have to think or dwell on it. Take it captive and replace it with the Word of God.

Armor of God

The battle for our lives is really fought in the mind. The good news is we do not have to fight this battle on our own. Paul tells us in Ephesians 6:10 to "A final word: Be strong in the Lord and in his mighty power." This cannot be accomplished if we do not know what the Bible says. This is why I am so passionate about reading, speaking and memorizing the word of God. The weapon of choice for us should be the Bible in this battle. God gave us the Word of God as a weapon against the devil. The Word of God is referred to as "the sword of the spirit" in Ephesians 6:17. Paul tells us in this passage to *take* the sword of the spirit which is the Word of God. Hebrews describes the Word of God like this, "For the word of God is alive and powerful. It is sharper than the sharpest two-edged sword, cutting between soul and spirit, between joint and marrow. It exposes our innermost thoughts and desires" (Hebrews 4:12). That is so powerful. This shows us that our battle is not impossible. Stop believing the devil's lies about you and let the Word of God change your mind. "So use every piece of God's armor to resist the enemy whenever he attacks, and when it is all over, you will still be *standing up*" (Ephesians 6:13 TLB). Yes! Be encouraged today that as you put on God's armor, you will be standing up and will not be defeated. A person who is still standing has not lost the fight.

Call to action:

What verse can you start memorizing to help you in this battle? Start with Romans 6:14 which says, "Sin is no longer your master…" When I finally understood this principle, it was life changing for me. Faith comes by hearing, so start memorizing a verse today. Print a verse or two out or write them on a 3x5 index card. If you will begin each week memorizing a verse or two it will help so much in the process of walking out your freedom. I started doing this and found by memorizing scripture it helped build me up spiritually. There was something that took place when I read these verses over and over out loud. We are going to talk about this several times throughout this book. It is imperative to overcoming any addiction or stronghold. It will also create a deeper love for the Bible and strengthen our relationship with God.

Practical step:

If your phone is a tool for you to look at porn, then do not sleep by it. Buy an alarm clock and leave your phone charging in a different room. Anything that you can do to give you time to think about your decision helps. It is ultimately your choice, but simple things can often times help us break a bad habit. If your phone is still the problem, then get a phone without the internet or lock out the internet until things improve. The choice is yours. At some point if you are married you have to let your wife know about your struggle. Let her set up a password to lock you out of the internet on your phone or computer. Your wife can be your ally when you allow her to be part of the healing process.

Discussion Questions:

1) Are you reading your Bible on a regular basis? If not, are you willing to make the commitment for the next thirty days to spend time reading your Bible? What adjustments do you need to make in your schedule in order for you

to spend some time each day reading and memorizing scripture?

_____
_____
_____
_____
_____
_____

2) What verses can you begin to write down and start to memorize?

_____
_____
_____
_____
_____
_____

Chapter 5

PRAYER CHANGES THINGS

*But when you pray, go away by yourself, all alone,
and shut the door behind you and pray
to your Father secretly, and your Father,
who knows your secrets, will reward you.*
--Matthew 6:6 TLB

Author and theologian R.C. Sproul said, "Prayer does change things, all kinds of things. But the most important thing it changes is us. As we engage in this communion with God more deeply and come to know the One with whom we are speaking more intimately, that growing knowledge of God reveals to us all the more brilliantly who we are and our need to change in conformity to Him. Prayer changes us profoundly."[19] Prayer is intentional communication with God and can be spoken or written. There are numerous types of prayers, but we will focus on a daily guide to prayer, praying the promises of God's Word and praying in the Spirit.

Daily Guide to Prayer

The most important thing a Christian can do on a daily basis is spend alone time with God. Jesus says, "Apart from Me you can do nothing…" (John 15:5 NIV). It goes on to say in John 15:6, "Anyone who does not remain in me is like a useless branch and withers." To wither means to dry up. If we do not take the time to seek God, we dry up spiritually. I need my time with God each day more than I need anything else. You will make time for what is most important in your life. As a Christian, our greatest desire should be to spend time alone with God on a consistent basis. I love to spend time early in the morning in prayer. Why early in the morning? Jesus modeled this example for us. Mark 1:35 says he "Before daybreak the next morning, Jesus got up and went out to an isolated place to pray." You don't have to do this, but I really challenge you to try it for thirty days and see what a difference it makes in your life. If I will take the time and sacrifice some sleep for prayer, my day goes so much better. So many times when I didn't know what to do I have gotten on my knees and sought the presence of God. Hebrews 4:16 (NKJV) says, "Let us therefore come boldly to the throne of grace, that we may obtain mercy and find grace to help in time of need."

When I finally got my life turned around, I was living in a little house with a drafty sunroom. I spent so many hours in that sunroom just praying. I was desperate for a change in my life and I poured my heart out to God. I would wake up early to seek God and it was in those times that I grew to know God so much more. To this day I still go to a room privately to pray. When I worked in the corporate world, I would often go to a park and pray in my car during lunch. Matthew 6:6 (TLB) tells us, "But when you pray, go away by yourself, all alone, and shut the door behind you and pray to your Father secretly, and your Father, who knows your secrets, will reward you." What we do in private affects our public life. According to this verse it really matters more what we do when no one is around. Start with any amount of time, then as you go along work on praying longer. The goal is not a certain amount of time. The goal is consistent daily time with God in prayer. James 4:8 says, "Come close to God, and God will come close to you." This is a promise from God that if we will take the time to draw near to Him, He will draw near to us.

In Matthew 5:9, Jesus gives us a guide for prayer. He said to pray like this: "Our Father in heaven, may your name be kept holy. May your Kingdom come soon. May your will be done on earth, as it is in heaven. Give us today the food we need, and forgive us our sins, as we have forgiven those who sin against us. And don't let us yield to temptation, but rescue us from the evil one." The book *Could You Not Tarry One Hour* by Pastor Larry Lea helped me in my prayer life. He has a prayer outline in the book based on the Lord's prayer which you can download from his website for free. There are also so many good books and materials to help you learn to pray. This part of the book only covers a small aspect on prayer, but it is vital to walking out your freedom.

Another aspect of prayer is waiting on the Lord. We talk to Him and then we listen for Him. Strong's Concordance defines waiting as stillness, quiet, trust, or silent.[20] It is so important to not only read our Bibles and speak the Word of God, but we also need to take the time to be silent with Him. Take the time to just sit and listen to God rather than to continually ask Him for something. It can be hard in our society, but we have to train ourselves to wait on God. We can learn to stop, put the cell phone down and quiet our mind before God. Sometimes what can help is journaling. Simply get out a notebook and pour out your heart and then listen for His still, small voice. Often while I am journaling, I am reminded of a verse and I write it down. Other times, God brings correction on areas I need to change in my life. In the book of Psalm, David talks about praising God and getting quiet before Him. "Let all that I am wait quietly before God, for my hope is in him" (Psalm 62:5).

There is something about praising God that reminds us of how great He is and how much He loves us. The Bible says, "Your unfailing love is better than life itself; how I praise you!" (Psalm 63:3).

Praying the promises

Praying the promises of God has been a key aspect of walking out my freedom. Matthew 24:35 says, "Heaven and earth will disappear, but my words will never disappear." God's Word is eternal. The Word of God is the will of God. So when we pray the Word, we are praying His will. Sometimes people say they do not know how to pray. Well, grab your Bible open it up and start praying Romans 6 or other passages from the Bible. I have already mentioned in this book about what reading Romans 6 has done for me. I literally would walk around our house and read Romans 6 out loud. I would be praying and then start quoting it. This got my focus off of the problem and turned my focus toward the solution. The answer for all of our daily struggles can be found in the Word of God. Isaiah 55:11 (NKJV) says, "So shall My word be that goes forth from My mouth;

It shall not return to Me void, But it shall accomplish what I please, And it shall prosper in the thing for which I sent it." Our words have power and when we pray the Word, things change. God created the earth with words and He created us in His image, so never underestimate the power of prayer.

2 Chronicles 16:9 (NKJV) says, "For the eyes of the Lord run to and fro throughout the whole earth, to show Himself strong on behalf of those whose heart is loyal to Him." He is going to work on your behalf. The word *strong* in this passage means courage, to fortify, or to conquer. That is what He will do on your behalf if you will believe His Word and obey it. My life has truly been changed by praying the Word. He is ready to perform a miracle in your life. He is just waiting for you to believe and seek Him.

"Then the Lord said to me, "You have seen well, for I am ready to perform My word."
—Jeremiah 1:12 NKJV

Praying the Ephesians Prayer

Praying the Ephesians prayers is something I do on a regular basis. At times throughout my week, I pray Ephesians 1:17-23 and Ephesians 3:14-21. This has helped me so much in my walk with God and with my journey in life. Ephesians 1:17 is asking God for spiritual wisdom and revelation. We need specific wisdom and revelation to know how to walk out our journey. There have been so many times I would walk around with my Bible open and speak these chapters out loud while I was praying. It is amazing what clarity comes to me for situations that I am facing daily because of reading the Ephesians prayers and listening to what the Holy Spirit is telling me. I love reading them specifically out of the Amplified version of the Bible. The Amplified version helps me understand this passage more clearly. My challenge to you is to open your Bible to these passages and speak them out loud as a prayer throughout your week and see what a difference it makes.

Praying in the Spirit

When you pray in tongues, you are speaking to God.[21] Praying in the spirit, unfortunately, has become controversial which I believe is a trick of the devil. He does not want you praying in the Spirit. Praying in the spirit builds us up; it gives us power and boldness. Jude 20 says, "But you, dear friends, must build each other up in your most holy faith, pray in the power of the Holy Spirit." Acts 1:8 (NKJV) says, "But you shall receive power when the Holy

Spirit has come upon you; and you shall be witnesses to Me in Jerusalem, and in all Judea and Samaria, and to the end of the earth." The word power[22] is defined as miraculous power, ability, might, and strength. Don't try to do it on your own. The Holy Spirit was given to us to help us. John 16:7 (NKJV) says, "Nevertheless I tell you the truth. It is to your advantage that I go away; for if I do not go away, the Helper will not come to you; but if I depart, I will send Him to you." In this battle you need all the help you can get, and the best help is the Holy Spirit.

Call to Action and Practical Steps:

Prayer was important to Jesus while He was on this earth, so it needs to be important to us too. Begin today by setting aside some time to pray. Find a park, go to your closet, garage, or wherever you can get alone with God. I am married and have three children and there are times I explain to them that dad is going to go pray for thirty minutes. This habit will not only help you walk out your thought life, but it will teach you to spend daily time with God.

Discussion Questions:

1) Have you developed a daily time in prayer with God?

_____
_____

2) What steps can you take to make sure that you are spending consistent time with God?

3) Is there something you need to sacrifice in your schedule to make sure you spend consistent time with God?

_____
_____
_____
_____
_____
_____

> *"Keep watch and pray, so that you will not give in to temptation. For the spirit is willing, but the body is weak!"*
>
> Matthew 26:41

Chapter 6

ACCOUNTABILITY — WHY AND WHAT IS IT?

"It is vital for our lives to have someone who can at anytime encourage, confront, or challenge us on our behavior and walk with God."
—*Jeff Goforth*

Accountability is a key part of staying free from sexual immorality. I view accountability as a multi-prong approach. If you are married, your wife can be your greatest ally. Sit down and have a few gut-level, honest talks. My advice is to have multiple conversations where you share portions of your struggles instead of unloading everything at once. Have your wife read the chapter my wife wrote at the end of the book. This will help her to understand how she can help in the area of accountability. This is a battle to be fought together.

The other prong is finding a same gender accountability partner. That might sound funny, but I believe accountability and counseling needs to be man to man and woman to woman. If you choose to skip this chapter or refuse to heed the warnings of being connected with others, then I promise you will not completely fulfill what God has for your life. It may sound harsh, but a week doesn't go by that I do not hear of another Christian who is caught up in some type of sexual immorality. If you could sit down with each one of them, likely they have two things in common. One: they are not truly accountable to someone else, and two: they stopped seeking God with all their heart (no fear of God). This does not have to be the case.

What steps are you taking to make sure you finish your Christian walk strong? God made us to fellowship with Him and to be connected with others. You need others helping you and they need your help. My life is so much richer now that I do not just live for myself. I have others in my life, who continually challenge me to finish strong. For many years I just lived to accumulate wealth and play golf. I had become very isolated. No one really knew what I was going through. Most men tend to try to go it alone, but this is a sure fire way to end up on the wrong path.

Isolation

Isolation means complete separation from others. Even in the midst of our 'connected' culture, I see so many men who are isolated. Humility is the key. I need others in my life in order to walk out this journey. If I isolate myself, I am a dead man. If I pull away from others, I know it's only a matter of time before I am going to be completely off track.

Are you isolated? Before you answer this I am not talking about how many 'friends' you have on Facebook or who is following you on social media. I am talking about someone who has permission to ask you tough questions on a regular basis about your thought life and your personal conduct. Based on that definition, are you isolated or connected?

You cannot do this journey alone! There are going to be times that you feel like quitting or you get tired of the struggle. You need others in your life who will call, text, take you to lunch and pray for you. This journey is about living life together and pushing each other towards the things of God. I have had several different people in my life over the years that have helped me in the area of accountability. Find someone of the same gender who will stick with you and help you on your journey. My wife definitely helps keep me accountable. Your spouse can become your greatest ally because once they know what you are struggling with they can help in the process. But I also have a guy I talk to on a regular basis to make sure I am staying on track.

The Amplified Bible says, "Two are better than one, because they have a good [more satisfying] reward for their labor; for if they fall, the one will lift up his fellow. But woe to him who is alone when he falls and has not another to lift him up! (Ecclesiastes 4:9-10 AMP). The New Living Translation says, "A person standing alone can be attacked and defeated, but two can stand back-to-back and conquer. Three are even better, for a triple-braided cord is not easily broken" (Ecclesiastes 4:12). I really like the way this translation says it because two standing back to back which means that they can help you see things that you do not see.

The bottom line is that we need other people in our lives. You need to find someone who will push you. There are times we need someone to push us to be better and rise above obstacles. I need it! I have not arrived to the point where I can do life by myself and neither have you.

It's easy to think you are not that far off track and really don't need anyone else in your life. If you get to this point, you are going to be in trouble before you know it. Even if you are a senior pastor, you still need someone to hold you accountable.

Pride

One of the biggest reasons we choose not to be connected to others is our pride. Pride keeps us from letting others know what we are going through. It keeps us from seeking out wise counsel from people we trust. It's not easy for any of us to trust someone with our personal struggles. It's even harder for men in leadership positions. I have seen too many pastors and church leaders get caught up in an affair because they weren't accountable to someone else on a regular basis.

I think the biggest reason why some men have problems getting an accountability partner is they do not feel like they can trust someone. You need to find someone you know who is going after God and who will keep your conversations private. In a class I took at my church, we were required to sign a confidentiality statement that we would not discuss what was said in our groups or what our accountability partners shared with us. I cannot stress the following statement enough:

DO NOT tell other people what your accountability partner tells you! TELL NO ONE, this includes your spouse! The only exception would be if someone tells you about an illegal activity.

The key is finding someone you trust. I tried it alone for years, and I told myself I did not need anyone else. I convinced myself that I could do it on my own. How did I do? Not very well at all. It's not easy to open up to someone else, but it is a critical pattern to build into your life to experience victory.

How to do Accountability

Here is how I do accountability with others. Depending on the situation, I normally try to talk to the person every other week. In some cases when things were more difficult, we would talk every week. Sometimes we talked on the phone, but I usually ask the person to meet with me face-to-face every other week. It's a lot harder to lie if they are sitting across the table from you. I know people have lied to me over the years, but that is their choice. In my own life I have my accountability partner ask me specific questions on things I have struggled with in the past. It is important to ask specific questions. Tell your accountability partner what questions that you want him to ask you.

I text each person that I am talking with regularly to see how they are doing. Sometimes we get together and we do not talk about anything serious. We go golfing or just hang out. It takes time for the relationship to develop so they can trust you. Again, DO NOT tell others what you talk about. Keep your conversations confidential. The only way I tell someone else is if they tell me they committed a crime. At that point you need to let them know that you have to inform the police. You may also need to tell the church leadership. The bottom line is, if they tell you something they did was illegal, you will be held responsible if you don't tell the authorities. Okay, that is the legal disclaimer, but it's an important one. You can end up in jail!

Accountability is such a key step in walking out your freedom. Why? There are times we all feel a pull to go back to a particular sin. I do not care how spiritual you think you are, you need others in your life who you feel comfortable with so you can tell them when you are struggling. Too many have tried to go it alone and they do not make it. Isolation for anyone is not good.

Mentoring and Discipleship

"Making disciples is all about seeing people transformed by the power of God's Word. If you want to see that happen in others, you need to be experiencing such transformation yourself."[23]
—Francis Chan

Your freedom is not just for you. A mentor is defined as someone who teaches or gives help and advice to a less experienced often younger person.[24] Discipleship is teaching people biblical principles and modeling how to walk those out in the real world. That is what this is all about. A spiritual mentor may not be someone who you have a personal relationship with, but they are contributing to your spiritual growth. In a discipleship relationship, you are more directly connected with someone on a personal level.

We all need to be disciple and to have mentors, but we should all be willing the help disciple and mentor others as well. Who can you help lead to Christ and then continue with them on their journey? Some men are so busy or they don't think they have what it takes to mentor or disciple others. We all should have a Paul, a Barnabas, and a Timothy in our lives. This example is from the New Testament and is a guide for us today. A Paul is someone who is mentoring you. It is someone you can go to with questions in life. It is someone who you can go to about what to do about a job, relationship questions, and someone to help train you spiritually to grow into a godly man. A Barnabas is someone who comes along side you and lives life with you. It's a peer relationship. This Barnabas is more of a friend who walks beside you. This godly friend will be someone who you share your life with. I have a very good friend named Chris who I met through golfing. He is a Barnabas in my life. We have met so many times for lunch, played golf, shared our dreams and struggles. My life has become so much richer because Chris has been in my life for so many years. A Timothy is someone you are pouring into, who is typically 10-15 years younger than you. You can be the person they go to when they have tough questions about relationships and who you can point to Christ. You are practically walking with them as they go through life. We all need each of these people in our lives.

Mentoring and discipleship are keys to a healthy walk with God. I can only imagine how much easier life would be for us all if each of us would find one to two people to do life with. We all have questions at times that we do not know who to ask. We all are going through things that we need help with at times. Will you be that person for someone else? I started doing this by accident when I finally turned my life back to Christ. I shared my testimony at church and someone heard it and wanted to meet with me. I did not think I had anything to offer someone else, but I wanted to help them if I could. After doing this for the last sixteen years, I have seen so much healing. I have seen many lives and marriages turned around. Sometimes I will meet with a person only once and it does not work out or continue for whatever reason. On some occasions though, I will meet and do life with a person for years. It's not because I know everything. To be honest, it's because I am willing to listen and give godly wisdom when I can. There are times I meet with a person and all we do is golf or go fishing. It is really about that person being able to trust you. When you take the time out of your busy schedule to meet for coffee or lunch it means a lot. The biggest lie is that you do not have what it takes to help someone else on their journey. You do have what it takes. Do not believe the devil's lie that you do not have anything that will help someone else.

The first place discipleship should be happening is in your own home. Before you go out to help the world, are you making yourself available to your own kids? What I have seen over the years is people trying to save the world yet they lose their kids in the process. That is not what God is asking from us.

There are many Christian men looking for someone to take the time be a spiritual father and help disciple them. We should be doing this because this is what Jesus was doing while He was on the earth. It's the ripple effect. You have no idea who the person you are mentoring today is going to become. You are changing a family and the generations to come. Is it always easy? No! Pouring into someone else takes time and it can get messy. Relationships take work, but in the end they are always worth it. I remember meeting with a young man for a couple of years and then he got married. We talked many times over coffee and on the golf course. He was working on overcoming some real struggles, but I watched him get through these things and get his life back on track. I had the honor of being in his wedding and afterwards received a thank you letter from his wife. She thanked me for taking the time to help her husband and said that I had helped shaped their family for years to come. Now to be honest so many times we met I would just listen and make myself available. There were times I brought correction and guidance, but many times I was just pointing him to Christ. I now have had the opportunity to meet with, live life with, and help support numerous young men.

Call to Action and Practical steps:

Make it a goal to find an accountability partner. Preferably, find someone who is already in your life. It might be someone at your church or a Christian co-worker. Do not be discouraged if you ask someone and they do not want to do it. Pray about who to ask and then reach out to that person and see if they would be willing to be an accountability partner. I have asked people who said they were too busy and I realized they were not the right person.

Here is a list of questions you can ask each other when you meet:

a) Have you been with anyone or anywhere that would or could appear compromising?

b) Have you entertained any inappropriate fantasies in your thought life?

c) Have you viewed or read any sexually explicit images or material?

d) How has your time with God been since the last time we spoke? Have you been reading the Bible? Praying?

You can use whatever questions you want, but it's good to give someone specific questions so they know what to ask you and you can do the same for them.

Discussion Questions:

1) Who can you ask to help keep you accountable?

_____

_____

2) If you are married have you talked to your spouse about helping you stay accountable while at home? _____

_____
_____
_____

3) Who can you reach out to and help them on their journey?

_____

_____

_____

Chapter 7

GAME PLAN FOR PRACTICAL STEPS

Now, it's time to get a game plan and get back in the race to finish strong. The Bible says, "I don't know about you, but I'm running hard for the finish line. I'm giving it everything I've got. No sloppy living for me! I'm staying alert and in top condition. I'm not going to get caught napping, telling everyone else all about it and then missing out myself" (1 Corinthians 9:26-27 MSG).

What extraordinary steps are you willing to take to make sure you finish strong? Here are some steps that have helped me and many others over the years. We have gone over most of these steps throughout the book but this list will help remind you of what to do.

1. **Set aside time in your schedule to be alone with God.** Plan out your schedule to spend daily time with God. It's not just going to happen if you don't plan it out. I often have my time with God in my car parked in a parking lot or a local park. We have three kids so I have to be creative. I prefer the morning because it sets the tone for my day. The bottom line is to just start making it a consistent daily habit.

2. **Read your Bible daily.** Buy a "one year" Bible that has a reading plan that allows you to read through it each year or use a Bible app to keep you on track. Many churches have a daily Bible reading plan. If you have trouble reading, then listen to an audio version. The important thing is to start getting the Word of God in you. There are also numerous daily Bible reading plans that are free online. (Note: You will find some links on the Resource page in the back of this book.)

3. **Memorize verses.** Get some scripture cards or write verses down on index cards and try to memorize a verse a week. Start somewhere. There are verses throughout this book that you can begin to think on and begin to memorize. Something powerful happens when we begin to memorize the Word of God. This was a big difference for me in my personal life and I still do it. I have

used 3x5 index cards and now I really like Moleskine® brand notebooks. I will work on one or two verses for several days and let it get deep in my thought life. As we know, our thoughts control our actions.

4. **Go to your local church and get plugged in.** Find where God wants you to go and stay planted. You need to hear what your preacher is teaching and let their Bible-based messages build up your faith. Too many people start to go to a church and get offended and leave. You have to make a decision that once you find the church God wants you to be in that you stay put.

5. **Give out of yourself.** This is such a key step in walking out your freedom and maintaining it. It takes the focus off of us and puts it on others. Depending on what you are walking out depends on how and where you can be involved at your church. Let the leadership of the church know what you are dealing with and they can find a place for you to give out.

6. **Stay accountable with someone.** There are going to be times you don't feel like seeking God or going to church. You need people in your life who are challenging you. Don't let pride stand in the way of this key step. Look back to the chapter on accountability if you have

questions on what it looks like. The bottom line is: do not isolate yourself.

7. **Leave your mobile phone plugged in away from where you sleep**. Night time can be a very difficult time in the beginning of walking this out. Give yourself extra steps to get to your phone at night. It makes you think about what you are doing by placing the phone in a different room while you sleep. This gives you time to change your mind and not make a mistake you will regret. If you use your phone for an alarm clock, then go buy a clock instead of using your phone. You might laugh at this, but too many men have been taken out by all the access they have at their fingertips.

8. **For a short time block the internet on your mobile phone or other devices**. I have advised guys to get an old phone with no internet service for a season of time. I did the same thing and it helped me break free of my addiction. Ultimately, you have to make the right choice. There will always be temptation around you, but if it helps to get rid of the internet for a season, then why not do it? I knew a guy who was given an iPad, but it was not helping him at all in his journey so he got rid of it. Sometimes you have to take radical steps to get free and stay free. There are also many internet filters

that can help you. I realize you can still access porn if you want to, but putting steps in your way to give you time to think is a huge help. You will pay the price if you continue looking at immoral images.

9. **Get plenty of rest**. Sleep is so important. This may seem very basic but you need sleep. I know when I am tired I do not handle things well. My flesh seems to want to take over. Your spirit man should control you. The flesh wants to control your actions, but you cannot let it. With God's help, this is not impossible. The Bible says, "So I run with purpose in every step. I am not just shadowboxing. I discipline my body like an athlete, training it to do what it should. Otherwise, I fear that after preaching to others I myself might be disqualified" (1 Corinthians 9:26-27).

10. **Exercise**. When you are dealing with sexual thoughts, go work out or go for a run. This helps in more ways than one—physically, mentally and emotionally. I tell guys all the time to go for a jog or hit the gym if they are struggling. Play a game of basketball with some friends, hit the golf course or do something physical that can help burn off some frustration.

11. **Stress.** Stress can come from work, family, finances or life in general. A bad day at work or a fight with a

spouse can end up with a bad decision. Our flesh wants to feel better. It does not like pain. Many people turn to alcohol, drugs, or pornography. Stress is a part of life. Some might say this is a bad confession, but it's the truth. We live in a world of constant demands. Decide ahead of time what you will do when you feel stressed – talk with your accountability partner or your wife, go for a run, play with your kids, read the Bible, or pray.

12. **Vacations, down time, or the holidays**. Vacations and holidays are a good thing, but when we are out of our routine we must be careful. Make a plan ahead of time on how you will spend your free time and how you will respond to temptation. You need to be aware of being out of your routine and make sure you stay accountable while you are away.

13. **Be careful how much time you are alone**. If you are married, and your wife is going out of town, have a plan of action. I have friends who had a friend stay with them, or they stayed at a relative's house during the time their spouse was gone. If you are single, then go hang out with some friends.

14. **Be careful how much media you take in and what kind**. DO NOT watch TV late at night by yourself. This kills the progress of many men. It reminds me of David

Game Plan for Practical Steps

from the Bible when he sinned with Bathsheba. He was at the wrong place at the wrong time. Do not make the same mistake. It cost him dearly. I personally don't watch any kind of movie, no matter what it is rated, if it has any kind of nudity. You can go to <u>dove.org</u> and they will tell you if there is anything in the movie that is not appropriate. I won't even watch PG-13 movies if there are sexually explicit scenes in the movie. It is not so much about the rating as it is about what images are going to be shown. When you take in those images, they stay with you. Don't make this mistake or you will regret it. I cannot tell you the number of movies I have had to turn off due to things in it that were immoral. The Bible says, "…A man reaps what he sows. The one who sows to please his sinful nature from that nature will reap destruction…" (Galatians 6:7-8 NIV).

15. **Train your eyes.** You may be in line at a store and a women may have an immodest top on and you have to train your eyes to look away. If an image comes on while watching a football game, you need to look away or turn the channel. As I have said, what we look at matters. The Bible says, "Turn away my eyes from looking at worthless things …" (Psalm 119:37 NKJV). What we allow ourselves to take in affects us. Images

looked at today can plant a seed in our minds that will produce an immoral action later on.

16. **Business Travel (Have a game plan).** You need to take extra steps when you are going to travel on business. What plan have you set up with your accountability partner? I have had people email me their itinerary to make sure I knew where they were going to be during their trip. This provides an extra layer of transparency with your accountability partner. Business travel can isolate you and you need to make sure you are prepared ahead of time. If at all possible, do not travel with a person of the opposite sex who is not your spouse.

17. **Get a filter for your all of your devices**. There are so many good options. Our website is jeffgoforth.org for more help.

18. **Block certain websites on your phone or computer.** If there is a website that continues to be a temptation, then block it in your settings and let someone else set the password.

19. **Be careful who you hang out with on a regular basis.** Who you spend time with on a regular basis will influence what you do. I have had friends over the years that were not good influences and I had to cut off

relationship with them because they kept trying to pull me back into things I did not want to do.

20. If you are in a dating relationship you need to have a plan set up to not be alone. This is not a book on dating, but too many people I know did not set up boundaries while they were dating. They then ended up crossing lines they regretted later on.

21. Don't take your phone in the bathroom. Don't laugh at this because this has really helped me over the years. You will be okay without your phone for a few minutes.

22. Keep your computer in a public space. Have your computer in a place where anyone can walk by and see what you are doing.

All of these are just suggestions that have helped me and others. Sometimes we have to take extraordinary steps to walk out our freedom.

> *"If you do well, will you not be accepted? And if you do not do well, sin crouches at your door; its desire is for you, but you must master it."*
>
> Genesis 4:7 AMP

Chapter 8

HELP FOR PARENTS

"Never before in the history of telecommunications media in the United States has so much indecent (and obscene) material been so easily accessible by so many minors in so many American homes with so few restrictions."[25]

— U.S. Department of Justice

My wife and I look at parenting like the greenhouse analogy. Young plants are brought into the warm and stable environment of a greenhouse to grow and then once they are strong and vibrant they are ready to be moved outdoors. However, you cannot simply place young plants in the greenhouse and expect them to grow. Tender plants must be cared for by providing rich soil, sunlight, water, fertilizer, protection from disease, and room to grow. Once these tender plants are properly cared for then they are better able to withstand the harsh elements outside of the greenhouse. This analogy can easily be related to how we raise our children. We welcome our children into our home and provide a stable environment by giving them all the elements they need to grow physically, emotionally, and spiritually until they are ready to face the world on their own. In this chapter we are going to tell you what has helped us with our children. We see our job as parents to prepare them so that when they come across things that are harmful they make godly decisions. As a parent you have to make some tough decisions. I realize that you cannot block everything from coming at your child, but there are certain things that they don't need access to until they are ready to make correct decisions. We have seen parents isolate their kids so much that they are not ready when they come of age, to make tough decisions. On the other hand, we have seen parents who have almost no restrictions. Parents are the gatekeepers of their families. A gatekeeper is the one in charge of passage through a gate, one who monitors or oversees the actions of others, and one who controls access to something, such as information or services.[26.] So how do we prepare our children? This is not an exhaustive list, but a balanced approach on how to be a gatekeeper for our children. As a parent we need to lead by example, create an open dialogue, and help navigate social and media decisions.

Lead by Example

The greatest thing we can do is lead by example. Our children watch us and see whether we practice what we preach. It's hard to talk to them about leading a life surrendered to God if we are not setting the example for them. If they see us up late watching filthy shows or movies and then we try to talk to them about what is right and wrong, then they will not respect what we are saying.

Ongoing Dialogue

The best communication happens when our children are willing to talk. Often that is at night or in the car driving somewhere. You may be tired, but take the time to listen. The best conversations I have had with my kids about difficult things have normally come at the worst time for me. I have had to choose to stop what I was doing and be willing to listen. Meaningful moments are never scheduled. They are captured.

What we have seen with our children over the years is that we have to be willing to communicate the "why's" of the boundaries we set for our kids. We also explain the benefits of boundaries. Boundaries are put in place to protect us. Each family has to decide what the boundaries will be in their home. For movies, our main concern is not the rating, but the content. Our overarching goal is to protect our kids from developing a sexual addiction, and part of our strategy is turning off movies that have overtly sexual images. Images are powerful and they stay with us longer than we realize. We have turned off many movies that we paid for because it just was not worth it to us. At that point, we treat it as a teaching moment and have a conversation with our kids to explain why we have this standard. This standard carries over to video games and music, but again, each parent has to decide the standards in their own home. It is so important to have an ongoing, open dialogue with your kids. They need to know they can tell you anything. Teach them to know God. Talk about spiritual things, have family devotions together, share areas where you have made mistakes. Deuteronomy 11:17:18 says, "So commit yourselves wholeheartedly to these words *(commands)* of mine. Tie them to your hands and wear them on your forehead as reminders. Teach them to your children. Talk about them when you are at home and when you are on the road, when you are going to bed and when you are getting up." This verse first shows how we have to commit to God's commands for our own life and then He tells us to talk to our children about them. He said to talk to them at home, on the road, going to bed, and when you are getting up. That means we have to talk to them all the time; whenever the moment presents itself. Sometimes parents are intimidated to talk to their children as they become teenagers. They need you even more when they are going through the teenage years to help them navigate difficult situations.

Friendships

As parents, we need to be careful who our children are communicating with online or in person. There are times our children have toxic friendships and we need to intervene to end any relationships that would be harmful to our children. At times when I was growing up my friends really had a greater influence in my life than my parents. It was a friend who exposed me to porn for the first time. I am not saying we isolate our children, but we must be aware who is influencing them.

Media

This section is difficult because of the complexities of our modern culture. With Facebook, Snapchat, Twitter,

Instagram, and all of the other social media outlets, the question comes: as parents what should we allow? Because of what we have overcome and helped others overcome, our boundaries are pretty tight. That does not mean our children are not on social media, but we have delayed access to certain sites until their spiritual and emotional maturity were ready to handle it. This is a really fluid topic because things change so quickly. We have noticed that each of our children handle things differently.

When it has come to cellphones, we have done different things. One of our sons accessed things on his phones at a younger age, so for a time we switched him to a phone without internet access. After a year or so, they were introduced to the smart phone with some apps, but restricted Safari. As more time went by the restrictions became fewer and fewer because we wanted to help him navigate things while he is in our home. If you restrict everything until they reach eighteen, then you run the risk of them not knowing how to handle technology. Our job is to prepare them for the real world. We tell our kids that right now we are setting their boundaries, but the time will come that they will have access to everything and they have to choose what they will look at and allow in their lives. We also have our kids plug their phones into a charging station downstairs, so that no phones go to their rooms at night. On that note, we also have not placed computers in our kids' rooms. The temptation is too great. We place our computers in open rooms so there is accountability for everyone. We could go into more depth, but we feel each parent needs to seek God for their own family. You are the gatekeeper for your children. Pray for wisdom and revelation on how to handle each these areas. These are formidable years and can ultimately determine their future.

Chapter 9

HELP FOR WIVES: YOU ARE ENOUGH
(A WORD FROM LISA GOFORTH)

So, your husband is addicted to porn? Maybe you have known, maybe you caught him, or maybe he just told you. What do you do now? Let me back up a bit and share my side of our story.

Jeff and I were college sweethearts who married our senior year of college. He was my soul mate and if I knew anything, it was that he was the perfect mate for me. There was never a doubt in my mind. We had similar upbringings; he was a pastor's kid and my parents were in ministry. We both had been saved at a young age, but we were not truly surrendered to the Lord. Our marriage was good on the surface for a few years, but deep cracks were forming below the surface.

About six years into our marriage, we had a son. What should have been a joyous time proved to be stressful and drew us further apart. He had started a corporate job and began going to happy hours in an attempt to climb the corporate ladder. I supported him 100%. Jeff is not one that does anything halfway. He is either all in or all out. He started staying out later and later and began taking business trips. I was naïve, but not completely stupid. I knew what was going on, but honestly did not want to admit anything. If I admitted it, then I would have to admit I was not enough for Jeff and that hurt. Slowly, I just started hardening my heart to him and began making plans in the back of my mind about how I would support my son and myself on my own.

Looking back, it is so sad how a hopeful marriage deteriorated into one that I did not even mind losing. I knew I was losing him, but I compartmentalized my emotions and convinced myself that I did not care. I was so hardened and deceived.

I distinctly remember when Jeff came home from a business trip and said he wanted to go to church. I was shocked at first because we had long before stopped going to church. Jeff went down to the altar and surrendered his life to the Lord. This was not just a rote prayer. This was a total surrender, never turning back, counting the cost and deciding the world did not have anything to offer. Like the Apostle Paul, it was his road-to-Damascus conversion. He would never be the same again.

We decided to sign up for a twelve week discipleship course at the church, which helped us start our communication and healing process. Jeff was so broken and began to share about what he was watching and the things that had transpired. Those were painful, but necessary conversations. We had multiple discussions when Jeff would share portions of information instead of unloading everything at once. I recommend taking it in small steps. Receiving all of the information at once can be overwhelming.

Caution: Some women want to know every detail. I caution you on that. Yes, you need to know things, but sometimes some of the details are unnecessary and only prove to create strongholds in your mind. Later on, it can be difficult to get past the wandering imaginations your mind creates.

This is why it is also important to have an accountability partner. Jeff found some men in leadership in the class that he was able to talk to, and they helped hold him accountable. I also had women I could talk to and seek counsel from. You both need support and encouragement as you walk through this process.

As we attended the discipleship class, I could see real changes in Jeff. I knew he needed help, but I did not realize how much help I needed. Somewhere during those twelve weeks my heart began to soften. My heart felt like dry, cracked ground where water poured off even though it desperately needed moisture. The Holy Spirit started tilling my heart, and I broke. I came to my end.

You Are Enough

I finally realized that no matter how perfect I might be, I was not meant to meet all of Jeff's needs. I was not designed to, and he was not designed to meet all of my needs. There are some needs in our soul that can only be touched by God. What a burden was lifted from our lives. This applies to you, too! You are enough to meet the needs of your husband that you were intended to meet.

I also realized that I was failing at the needs I could meet. I began reading *The Five Love Languages* by Gary Chapman. It was such an eye opener at the time. Jeff and I are so similar, yet our love languages are different. Is food a love language? Ha! No, but if it was then that would be Jeff's. His main love language is acts of service. I was definitely not showing him love by the language he understood. I wanted to spend time with him, which was my love language. I always thought it was so odd how excited he got when I made a great meal, ironed his clothes, or picked up his dry cleaning. I thought those things were kind of boring, but come to find out that's exactly what communicated my love to Jeff in his love language. Many marriages have been saved from the brink of divorce by just one person in the marriage learning to express their spouse's love language. Trust me, before long it will be reciprocated.

Protecting Your Eyes

Taking practical steps, we began to rebuild our marriage bit by bit. We took time to discuss and set our boundaries. One of our practical steps was getting rid of our personal computer (this was before filtering services) and choosing not to watch certain movies. We were not being legalistic about this. Visual images are powerful, so we wanted to protect what we allowed ourselves to see. The Bible says, "I will refuse to look at anything vile and vulgar" (Psalm 101:3).

Protecting our eyes is so important for pure thinking. According to the Bible, we can choose our thoughts, so must guard what we read and see, which is where our thoughts come from. The Bible says, "And now, dear brothers and sisters, one final thing. Fix your thoughts on what is true, and honorable, and right, and pure, and lovely, and admirable. Think about things that are excellent and worthy of praise" (Philippians 4:8). Most of us are not trained to protect what we allow through our "eye gates." I had not protected myself from immoral images either. I was so naive to how sexually immoral images can distort our view of sex and I had to dive into the scriptures and renew my mind right along with Jeff.

Renewing your mind is the process of displacing your old thoughts and replacing them with new thoughts. We have to use the word of God to displace our old, immoral thoughts with life giving scriptures. Anytime negative or fearful thoughts try to come your way, recite 1 Corinthians 10:3-5 with an emphasis on the last part of verse 5. Taking those thoughts captive and making them obedient to Christ. "For though we live in the world, we do not wage war as the world does. The weapons we fight with are not the weapons of the world. On the contrary, they have divine power to demolish strongholds. We demolish arguments and every pretension that sets itself up against the knowledge of God, and we take captive every thought to make it obedient to Christ" (2 Corinthians 10:3-5 NIV).

Help for Wives: You Are Enough (A word from Lisa Goforth)

No matter how you found out about your husband's pornography addiction, remember that your world might be rocked, but nothing has initially changed for your husband. He might have come clean, but these are things he has lived with and gotten used to for years. There will be a wide range of emotions, starting with shock, hurt, and leading to anger. If your husband told you what was going on, be thankful he was honest with you. Many men never really tell their wives the truth. If you found out, well, that can be good, too. It will force a confrontation and a decision on how to proceed.

Forgiveness

Sometimes people feel the need to withhold forgiveness because they feel if they forgive then that gives the other person a pass and it does not punish them. They also feel the act of forgiving gives the person a license to hurt them again. We will all be in a position to need forgiveness and the Bible commands us to forgive others in order to receive forgiveness for ourselves. "If you forgive those who sin against you, your heavenly Father will forgive you. But if you refuse to forgive others, your Father will not forgive your sins" (Matthew 6:14-15).

God can help us release our hurt. That being said, there is a practical side to this as well. You may need to have medical testing for STDs before intimacy if there was infidelity. If there is abuse, you need to talk with a godly woman, counselor, or family therapist. There are many forms of addiction to pornography. I highly recommend reading *Pulling Back the Shades: Erotica, Intimacy, and the Longings of a Woman's Heart* by Dr. Juli Slattery & Dannah K. Gresh. Their expert advice addresses godly intimacy issues that are usually not talked about in families or the church.

INTIMACY

Be sensitive to the sexual needs of your marriage. God created sexual intimacy to be enjoyed. If you have an unholy view of sex (and I believe most of us do because of the way the devil has used the media to pervert it), then ask the Lord to renew your mind. Find scriptures to help you fix your mind on things that are pure. The Bible says, "Everything is pure to those whose hearts are pure. But nothing is pure to those who are corrupt and unbelieving, because their minds and consciences are corrupted" (Titus 1:15).

Help for Wives: You Are Enough (A word from Lisa Goforth)

Communicate freely with your husband about intimacy, including your likes and dislikes. Pay attention to your husband, flirt with him, and invest in your relationship. Is your dog more excited to see your husband when he returns from work than you are? Greet him, hug him, and show him that you care. Yes, you are probably tired, but it can be the small things that make such a difference. Give it time. I am sure your husband will begin to respond in kind.

When we are married, we give ourselves freely to each other. The Bible says, "The husband should fulfill his wife's sexual needs, and the wife should fulfill her husband's needs. The wife gives authority over her body to her husband, and the husband gives authority over his body to his wife. Do not deprive each other of sexual relations, unless you both agree to refrain from sexual intimacy for a limited time so you can give yourselves more completely to prayer. Afterward, you should come together again so that Satan won't be able to tempt you because of your lack of self-control" (1 Corinthians 7:3-5). Do not use sex as a tool to manipulate or punish your husband. Do not refuse sex unless there are real physical reasons behind your refusal. Continual rejection is hurtful to both men and women. Initiate intimacy with your husband. It can take many years for things to work like clockwork in your sex life. Enjoy that time figuring out likes and dislikes together and be patient with yourselves.

I found that intimacy was very different after we truly surrendered our lives to the Lord. My attitude toward sex changed. I started viewing it as a way to please my husband and not just to gain pleasure for myself. Also, when you are both surrendered to the Lord, you are joined on a different level. We are spiritual beings with a spirit, a soul, and a body. Anyone can have a physical relationship, but when you are married and both surrendered to the Lord there is a spiritual intimacy. I began to really know the essence of who Jeff was and connected with him differently. Intimacy is deeper and more intense.

I am not an expert, but I have walked this out. Was it easy? No. But I have watched God heal my heart, set us free from immoral thoughts, help us learn how to love each other in a godly way, and create a marriage fully devoted to God.

Are you ready for a change in your marriage? Focus on these steps:

1. **Have the ugly talk.** I mean the gut-level, honest talk. Be honest with him and ask him to be honest with you. You do not need to know everything in one setting,

but listen and guard your heart. Some things might be quite hurtful to hear, but it's better to know and then deal with it. Encourage your husband to find a male accountability partner, and I encourage you find a godly woman for accountability.

2. **Humble yourself before God.** Pour your heart out to Him. He knows it all anyway. He will never leave you nor forsake you.

3. **Surrender your life to the Lord.** Surrender your will and your future. A surrendered heart seeks to please the Father and do His will. "Then Jesus said to his disciples, 'If any of you wants to be my follower, you must turn from your selfish ways, take up your cross, and follow me'" (Matthew 16:24). At the end of your life, you will stand before the Father to give an account of your life. You can't point to others as an excuse for how you lived your life. The Bible says, "So then, each of us will give an account of ourselves to God" (Romans 14:12 NIV). "For we must all stand before Christ to be judged. We will each receive whatever we deserve for the good or evil we have done in this earthly body" (2 Corinthians 5:10). Sobering, isn't it? Regardless of what your husband does, you must seek God for yourself. The Bible says, "Search for him and you will find

him. Then [with a deep longing] you will seek Me and require Me [as a vital necessity] and [you will] find Me when you search for Me with all your heart" (Jeremiah 29:13 AMP).

4. **Read the *Five Love Languages* by Gary Chapman and start applying the principles right away.**

5. **Partner with your husband in the struggle.**

Download a filtering service for your phones and/or computer.

Protect what you watch because men are even more visual than women. There are many television programs or movies we choose not to watch that contain sexual content or immoral images. There are many reality shows and movies that are full of immoral behavior and when you are contending for your marriage you do not want to allow those programs in your home. A good plot isn't worth temptation. Gain an eternal perspective. It's just a movie or a TV show. Is it worth your marriage? If you are raising children, you need to protect their eye gates too.

Be a partner, not a personal Holy Spirit by trying to tell him what to do all the time. Pray for your husband, believe in him, fulfill his sexual needs, walk in love with him, be kind, and allow time for trust to build.

6. **Work on developing intimacy and rebuilding trust.** Make love often. Read *Pulling Back the Shades Erotica, Intimacy, and the Longings of a Woman's Heart* by Dr. Juli Slattery & Dannah K. Gresh. Find a godly woman you can talk to if you have questions.

7. **Read your Bible every day.** It sounds simplistic, but by just reading your Bible you will grow in your faith and relationship with God. The word of God is alive, it's not just a book. "For the word of God is alive and powerful. It is sharper than the sharpest two-edged sword, cutting between soul and spirit, between joint and marrow. It exposes our innermost thoughts and desires" (Hebrews 4:12).

8. **Pray every day.** Prayer is simply talking to God. It does not need to be formal. God knows you. He knows your thoughts. Talk to him. Cast your cares on him. When we spend time with God, we take on His nature. Need peace or joy? Spend time with the Father.

    a. "Give all your worries and cares to God, for he cares about you" (1 Peter 5:7).

b. "Don't be afraid, for I am with you. Don't be discouraged, for I am your God. I will strengthen you and help you. I will hold you up with my victorious right hand" (Isaiah 41:10).

c. "I will be your God throughout your lifetime—until your hair is white with age. I made you, and I will care for you. I will carry you along and save you" (Isaiah 46:4).

9. **Find scriptures to stand on for your husband and yourself.** Here's a few to get you started:

Insert your name and then your husband's name for *love* in the following passage:

"Love is patient and kind. Love is not jealous or boastful or proud 5 or rude. It does not demand its own way. It is not irritable, and it keeps no record of being wronged. It does not rejoice about injustice but rejoices whenever the truth wins out. Love never gives up, never loses faith, is always hopeful, and endures through every circumstance" (1 Corinthians 13:4-8).

"For God did not give us a spirit of timidity or cowardice or fear, but [He has given us a spirit] of power

and of love and of sound judgment and personal discipline [abilities that result in a calm, well-balanced mind and self-control]" (2 Timothy 1:7 AMP).

"Do not conform to the pattern of this world, but be transformed by the renewing of your mind. Then you will be able to test and approve what God's will is—his good, pleasing and perfect will" (Romans 12:2 NIV).

"So kill (deaden, [a]deprive of power) the evil desire lurking in your members [those animal impulses and all that is earthly in you that is employed in sin]: sexual vice, impurity, sensual appetites, unholy desires, and all greed and covetousness, for that is idolatry (the deifying of self and other created things instead of God). It is on account of these [very sins] that the [holy] anger of God is ever coming upon the sons of disobedience (those who are obstinately opposed to the divine will), among whom you also once walked, when you were living in and addicted to [such practices]" (Colossians 3:5-7 AMPC).

"Do you not know that your bodies are temples of the Holy Spirit, who is in you, whom you have received from God? You are not your own; you were

bought at a price. Therefore honor God with your bodies" (1 Corinthians 6:19-20 NIV).

"And now, dear brothers and sisters, one final thing. Fix your thoughts on what is true, and honorable, and right, and pure, and lovely, and admirable. Think about things that are excellent and worthy of praise" (Philippians 4:8).

10. **Be faithful.** Read Proverbs 31 with an emphasis on verse 30. "Charm and grace are deceptive, and [superficial] beauty is vain, but a woman who fears the Lord [reverently worshiping, obeying, serving, and trusting Him with awe-filled respect], she shall be praised" (Proverbs 31:30).

Galatians 5:1 says "It is for freedom that Christ set us free." Being free implies not being in bondage. These steps can be difficult and will take time, but freedom lies on the other side. Pursue and contend for your freedom.

A Note from the Author

Change the way you think and it will change the way you live. "Don't become so well-adjusted to your culture that you fit into it without even thinking. Instead, fix your attention on God. You'll be changed from the inside out."[27] This is our prayer for you that you will be changed from the inside out. Allow God's Word to transform the way you think, so you will change the way you live.

Contact Information

We are here to help you on your journey. If this book has ministered to you, or if we can pray with you or answer questions, please contact us. We would love to hear from you.

Website is: jeffgoforth.org
E-mail is goforthmin@mac.com
Ministry phone: (918)402-6088

No test or temptation that comes your way is beyond the course of what others have had to face. All you need to remember is that God will never let you down; he'll never let you be pushed past your limit; he'll always be there to help you come through it.

1 Corinthians 10:13 MSG

ABOUT THE AUTHOR

In 2000, Jeff Goforth came to the end of himself in a hotel room in New Orleans. After running from God for many years, he had an encounter with Him that night. Jeff became desperate for a change in his life. The years of pornography and alcohol addiction had taken their toll on his life and marriage. After that night he would never be the same again. The journey that began that night set in motion a six-year period of seeking God and getting free. After sharing his testimony, men began to contact him about their struggles. Jeff had the opportunity to help numerous believers walk out their freedom.

God gave Jeff the idea to produce scripture CD's to help those struggling with the same issues. The first CD was "Renew: Change Your Mind," followed by "Fear Not," "Walking In Love," and "Nothing is Impossible with God." Over the past ten years, thousands of CD's have been sold and gone around the world helping people get freedom in their thought lives. Jeff worked in the corporate world for eighteen years trading natural gas. He would meet with men while working in the corporate world, but had a desire to pursue ministry full time. In addition to this book, Jeff is the author of *Fear Not,* which is his journey on getting free from panic attacks and anxiety. As an additional resource, Jeff Goforth Ministries has weekly podcasts, blogs, and online classes to help people on their journey to freedom. He also travels around the world teaching people the principles he learned on how to be free in their thought lives as well as how to be transformed by the Word of God.

Jeff and his wife, Lisa, have been married for twenty-three years. They reside in Tulsa, Oklahoma, and are the parents of three children.

SCRIPTURES TO HELP YOU

For though we walk in the flesh, we do not war according to the flesh. For the weapons of our warfare are not carnal but mighty in God for pulling down strongholds, casting down arguments and every high thing that exalts itself against the knowledge of God, bringing every thought into captivity to the obedience of Christ.

2 Corinthians 10:3-5 (NKJV)

But you have not so learned Christ, if indeed you have heard Him and have been taught by Him, as the truth is in Jesus: that you put off, concerning your former conduct, the old man which grows corrupt according to the deceitful lusts, and be renewed in the spirit of your mind, and that you put on the new man which was created according to God, in true righteousness and holiness.

Ephesians 4:20-24 (NKJV)

I beseech you therefore, brethren, by the mercies of God, that you present your bodies a living sacrifice, holy, acceptable to God, which is your reasonable service. And do not be conformed to this world, but be transformed by the renewing of your mind, that you may prove what is that good and acceptable and perfect will of God.

Romans 12:1-2 (NKJV)

My son, give attention to my words; Incline your ear to my sayings. Do not let them depart from your eyes; Keep them in the midst of your heart; for they are life to those who find them, and health to all their flesh. Keep your heart with all diligence, for out of it spring the issues of life.

Proverbs 4:20-23 (NKJV)

For as he thinks in his heart so is he.

Proverbs 23:7 (NKJV)

Therefore do not let sin reign in your mortal body, that you should obey it in its lusts. And do not present your members as instruments of unrighteousness to sin, but present yourselves to God as being alive from the dead, and your members as instruments of righteousness to God. For sin shall not have dominion over you, for you are not under law but under grace.

Romans 6:12-14 (NKJV)

Having disarmed principalities and powers, He made a public spectacle of them, triumphing over them in it.

Colossians 2:15 (NKJV)

"Enter by the narrow gate; for wide is the gate and broad is the way that leads to destruction, and there are many who go in by it. Because narrow is the gate and difficult is the way which leads to life, and there are few who find it.

Matthew 7:13-14 (NKJV)

Let there be no sexual immorality, impurity, or greed among you. Such sins have no place among God's people. Obscene stories, foolish talk, and coarse jokes—these are not for you. Instead, let there be thankfulness to God. You can be sure that no immoral, impure, or greedy person will inherit the Kingdom of Christ and of God. For a greedy person is an idolater, worshiping the things of this world.

Ephesians 5:3-5

We know that our old sinful selves were crucified with Christ so that sin might lose its power in our lives. We are no longer slaves to sin.

Romans 6:6

Run from sexual sin! No other sin so clearly affects the body as this one does. For sexual immorality is a sin against your own body. Don't you realize that your body is the temple of the Holy Spirit, who lives in you and was given to you by God? You do not belong to yourself, for God bought you with a high price. So you must honor God with your body.

1 Corinthians 6:18-20

Finally, dear brothers and sisters, we urge you in the name of the Lord Jesus to live in a way that pleases God, as we have taught you. You live this way already, and we encourage you to do so even more. For you remember what we taught you by the authority of the Lord Jesus. God's will is for you to be holy, so stay away from all sexual sin. Then each of you will control his own body and live in holiness and honor.

> 1 Thessalonians 4:1-4

…But the Son of God came to destroy the works of the devil.

> 1 John 3:8

You are of God, little children, and have overcome them, because He who is in you is greater than he who is in the world.

> 1 John 4:4 (NKJV)

For God has not called us to be dirty-minded and full of lust but to be holy and clean. If anyone refuses to live by these rules, he is not disobeying the rules of men but of God who gives his Holy Spirit to you.

> 1 Thessalonians 4:7-8 (TLB)

Resources
Recommended Books and Helps

Truly Free by Robert Morris

Battlefield of the Mind by Joyce Meyer

Dressed To Kill by Rick Renner

Model Man by Pastor Larry Stockstill

Finishing Strong by Steve Farar

Bible, Devotions and Study Helps - www.biblegateway.com

www.celebraterecovery.com

Christian movie review site - www.dove.org

Conquer Series - conquerseries.com

Larry Lea Prayer Outline - larrylea.com

Filters:

You can go to jeffgoforth.org for filter resources.

NOTES

Chapter 1 My Journey
[1] Covenant Eyes. Porn Stats. http://www.covenanteyes.com/?s=9+out+of+10+boys+are. Accessed June 5, 2016.
[2] Covenant Eyes. Porn Stats. http://www.covenanteyes.com/pornstats/. Accessed June 5, 2016.
[3] Ibid.

Chapter 2 God's Standard for Our Lives
[4] NIV
[5] Dictionary.com Unabridged. Random House, Inc. http://www.dictionary.com/browse/hint. Accessed June 5, 2016.

Chapter 3 The Fear of the Lord Produces Holiness
[6] Tozer, A.W. *Tozer Devotional.* The Christian and Missionary Alliance. https://www.cmalliance.org/devotions/tozer?id=1379 Accessed July 15, 2016.
[7] Vine, W. E., Merrill F. Unger, and William White. Vine's Complete Expository Dictionary of Old and New Testament Words: With Topical Index, Thomas Nelson Publishers, Nashville, TN. 1996.
[8] Daugherty, Billy Joe. *The Fear of the Lord.* Victory Press, Tulsa, OK. 1990. page 2
[9] Elwell, W. A., & Beitzel, B. J. Encyclopedia of the Bible. Grand Rapids, MI: Baker Book House, Grand Rapid, Michigan. 1988. page 984
[10] Collins English Dictionary – Complete and Unabridged, 12th Edition 2014. (1991, 1994, 1998, 2000, 2003, 2006, 2007, 2009, 2011, 2014). http://www.thefreedictionary.com/self-control. Accessed June 5 2016
[11] Elwell, W. A., & Elwell, W. A. Evangelical Dictionary of Biblical Theology (electronic edition). Baker Book House, Grand Rapids, MI. 1996. Accessed June 5, 2016

[12] Litwak, K. D., D. Mangum, D. R. Brown, R. Klippenstein, & R. Hurst (Eds.), Lexham Theological Wordbook. Lexham Press, Bellingham, WA. 2014.

Chapter 4 Change Your Mind - Allowing God's Word to Change You

[13] Daugherty, Billy Joe, *Renewing Your Mind*. Victory Press, Tulsa, OK. 1995. page 15

[14] Philippians 4:8

[15] Strong, James, *The Comprehensive Concordance of the Bible: Together with Dictionaries of the Hebrew and Greek Words of the Original, with References to the English Words*. World Bible Press, Iowa Falls, IA. 1988. page 65.

[16] Merriam-Webster.com. http://www.merriam-webster.com/dictionary/meditate. Accessed June 6, 2016.

[17] North Shore Community College, *Memory Concentration Recall Memory Tips*, North Shore Community College. Danvers, MA. https://www.northshore.edu/advising/pdf/memory.pdf Accessed July 10, 2016.

[18] NKJV

Chapter 5 Prayer Changes Things

[19] Lowery, D. D., Lexham Theological Wordbook. Lexham Press. Bellingham, WA. 2014.

[20] Strong, James, *The Comprehensive Concordance of the Bible: Together with Dictionaries of the Hebrew and Greek Words of the Original, with References to the English Words*. World Bible Press, Iowa Falls, IA. 1988. 31.

[21] Daugherty, Billy Joe. *Principles of Prayer*. Victory Press, Tulsa, OK. 1996.

Chapter 6 Accountability - Why and What is it?

[22] Strong, James, *The Comprehensive Concordance of the Bible: Together with Dictionaries of the Hebrew and Greek Words of the*

Original, with References to the English Words. World Bible Press, Iowa Falls, IA. 1988. page 24.

[23] Chan, Francis. *The Heart of a Disciple Maker.* https://exponential.org/francis-chan-do-you-have-the-heart-of-a-disciple-maker/ Accessed July 8, 2016.

[24] Merriam-Webster.com. *Merriam-Webster Dictionary.* http://www.merriam-webster.com/dictionary/mentor. Accessed June 6, 2016.

Chapter 8 Help for Parents

[25] Covenant Eyes, *Porn Stats.* Department of Justice. http://www.covenanteyes.com/pornstats/.Accessed, July 8, 2016.

[26] *The American Heritage® Dictionary of the English Language*, 5th edition. Houghton Mifflin Harcourt Publishing Company, Boston, MA. 2013

[27] Romans 12:2 MSG

Scripture Series

f jeffgoforthministries

🐦 jeffmgoforth

✉ mail@jeffgoforth.org

jeffgoforth.org